Tools of
4 *Emotional*
HEALING

D1565529

Tools of
4 *Emotional*
HEALING

Honesty, Forgiveness, Compassion & Faith

Justice Saint Rain

Book 2 of the
Love, Lust and the Longing for God trilogy,
which includes:
The Secret of Emotions
&
Longing for Love

SPECIAL ♥ IDEAS

Special Ideas
511 Diamond Rd Heltonville IN 47436
1-800-326-1197

4 Tools of Emotional Healing
By Justice Saint Rain

This book may be purchased individually at
Amazon.com or purchased both individually and in bulk at
www.secretofemotions.com or www.interfaithresources.com

Other books by Justice Saint Rain

The Secret of Emotions
Why Me? A Spiritual Guide to Growing Through Tests
The Secret of Happiness
A Spiritual Guide to Great Sex
Falling Into Grace
My Bahá'í Faith
The Hard Way – Lessons Learned
from the Economic Collaps

Printed in the USA

ISBN 978-1888547-52-8

To all of the people who are ready to
be honest with themselves
to forgive themselves
to have compassion
for themselves and others
and to have faith that things
really can get better.

꧁

Introduction

Though they are not quite the four horsemen of the apocalypse, the painful emotions of shame, anger, loneliness and fear have destroyed countless lives. The need to numb and distract ourselves from them leads us to engage in behaviors that only draw us deeper into shame and isolation. We do not need distractions or drugs, we need healing. Healing is not about solving our problems; it is about making us whole.

The qualities of honesty, forgiveness, compassion and faith can ease the pain of these emotions by filling the empty spaces they represent.

When we are in severe physical pain, many of us will immediately seek out medical help in order to diagnose the problem and gain some kind of relief. Some of us, however, will avoid asking for help for a variety of reasons. Perhaps we were taught that sickness is a sign of weakness and so we feel ashamed when we are sick or hurt. Many will choose denial to try and convince themselves the pain isn't that bad after all. Others will admit that they are in pain, but cling to a false hope that the pain will just go away on its own. Some will dread getting help for fear that the diagnosis will prove terminal, or will cause them to lose some part of themselves.

People's response to emotional pain is often similar. Whether it is the result of depression, addictions, unhealthy relationships or compulsive behaviors, many of us will delay seeking help for as long as we can. We will allow shame, denial, false hope and fear to drive us over the cliff of despair before we finally hit bottom and acknowledge that we can't overcome our pain on our own.

It doesn't have to be that way.

No law says that you have to hit bottom before seeking help, any more than you have to be on your death bed before calling for a doctor. If something causes you emotional pain or discomfort, and you don't know how to resolve it, go get help.

You can start here.

This book is not designed to replace the help you can receive from an appropriate twelve-step group or professional therapist. It is, instead, a way to jump-start your emotional healing process by introducing four core character strengths (also known as virtues) that will prepare you for the healing process. Whether you gather up the courage to walk into a twelve-step meeting, make an appointment for a private therapy session, or schedule a trip to a treatment center, understanding the importance of honesty, forgiveness, compassion and faith will give you a solid foundation for whatever healing work you need to do. These four tools address the universal challenges of shame, anger, loneliness and fear. They are tools that can transform your life and ease your pain. There are many other virtues that can build on this foundation, but these are an important place to start.

This is book two in the series *Love, Lust and the Longing for God*. Book one, *The Secret of Emotions*, introduced some helpful concepts that I will review now. It will just take a few minutes to explain the basics. If they seem more important to you right now than the four tools that this book talks about, you might want to read it first. But if you think you understand the ideas and are ready to tackle the goals of honesty, forgiveness, compassion and faith, then dive in. You can always go back and read the first book later.

The Secret of Emotions

Most of our actions are guided more by our emotions than our reason, and yet few people understand the nature of emotions or what emotional sensations are trying to tell us. We follow the promptings of our heart without understanding its language. In fact, the more sure we are that we know what we are feeling, the more likely it is that we are completely confused.

This is not our fault. How can we be expected to understand a language that neither we nor any of our family, friends or teachers have been taught?

In order to understand the language of the heart, I offer a simple observation:

The words associated with positive emotional sensations, such as hope, kindness, enthusiasm, gratitude, wonder and others, are also the words we use to name virtues. In fact, here is a whole list of positive emotions named after the virtues that are present when we feel them:

Compassion	Grace	Nobility
Confidence	Gratitude	Optimism
Contentment	Happiness	Patience
Courage	Hope	Peace
Creative	Honesty	Perseverance
Determination	Humility	Radiance
Empathy	Initiative	Resilience
Enthusiasm	Integrity	Respect
Faith	Joy	Reverence
Forgiveness	Kindness	Serenity
Friendship	Love	Strength
Generosity	Loyalty	Wonder
Gentleness	Modesty	

Surrounding ourselves with these virtues, whether it is in the friends we keep or the qualities we practice, feels good. Conversely, when we are feeling a positive emotion, we are probably in the presence of a virtue. Our emotions are messengers that tell us about our spiritual environment.

Negative emotions, then, tell us when these virtues and others are absent. Anger tells us that we perceive a lack of justice. Fear tells us we lack security. Shame tells us that we were not treated with nobility. The feelings we carry with us from our childhood tell us the qualities that were missing in our early lives.

These feelings are messengers. Instead of clinging to them when they are good, or hiding from them when they are bad, we can learn from them. They tell us which virtues we love, and they tell us which virtues are missing.

When we know what is missing in our lives, we can go out and get it.

It feels bad to have been raised without love, without nobility and without security. That is why many of us have tried to use physical sensations or physical drugs to dull the spiritual pain of sorrow, shame and fear. But there is an alternative. We can create what was missing rather than distract ourselves from the pain of its loss. Life is not an either/or choice between pain and emptiness. There is a third choice. Positive emotions—generated by practicing virtues and surrounding ourselves with virtuous people—feel good.

This, in a nutshell, is the message of *The Secret of Emotions*—that emotions tell us about the presence or absence of virtues in our lives and, instead of struggling with our painful emotions, we can choose to replace them with positive sensations. These positive emotions aren't created through mental discipline or wishful thinking, but are generated by the development of our own spiritual potential expressed in the practice of virtues.

This book is built on the belief that the virtues that we are longing for are the qualities of the Divine that were placed in our hearts by a loving God. You do not have to believe in God or the divine nature of emotional healing in order to benefit from the program I outline, but if you can at least consider a role for a Higher Power in the healing process, it will infuse your efforts with a measure of hope and joy.

Four Tools of Emotional Healing is about four specific virtues that can help heal the most common sources of emotional pain. They replace the pain of shame, anger, loneliness and fear with honesty, forgiveness, compassion and faith. At the same time, they lay the foundation for many other virtues and the positive emotional sensations that go with them.

Acknowledgements

Many thanks to the people who read early copies of this work and gave invaluable feedback: Phyllis Edgerly Ring, editor, and the author of *Life at First Sight – Finding the Divine in the Details*; Phyllis K. Peterson, author of *Remaining Faithful*; Kim Bowden-Kerby, whose advice was worth much more than I paid for it; and Jay Cardwell who found more in it than I put in.

Thanks, also, to all of the readers of my earlier works whose support and encouragement made the publication of this book possible.

Healing What Is Missing

The emotional pain caused by shame, anger, loneliness and fear is a message telling us that there is something missing in our lives.

What is missing is honest self-knowledge, forgiveness, compassion and faith.

It is not our fault.

We can't be expected to have developed qualities that we were never shown as children, any more than we could be expected to know how to swim if we had never been taken to a lake or pool.

The question is, now that we are adults and can recognize the skills we lack, do we hide our heads in shame, or make a conscious effort to acquire them?

I will be blunt. Honesty, forgiveness, compassion and faith are what many people would call virtues, and virtues have been given a pretty bum rap lately. Even psychologists who study them for a living prefer to use the code words "character strengths" to refer to these positive qualities because no one wants to be asked to become "virtuous." People reviewing my books have even told me that they would sell much better if I could just find a better word to use.

Here's why:

Virtues have often been spoken of as though they were burdens. They were seen as effort you put forth on behalf of someone else—to make *their* lives better, not yours. To be honest, for example, was to lose the advantage of deceit. To forgive was to let go of revenge and become a victim. Compassion meant taking care of others at your own expense, and faith was something you had to feign in order to please an angry God.

But let me offer another perspective:

Honest people like themselves.

Forgiving people are at peace with themselves and the world.

Compassionate people feel connected rather than isolated and alone.

People with faith in the goodness of life are not afraid of the world.

These virtues are not obligations to anyone else. They are qualities that can fill the empty places in your life. They are the greatest gifts you can give yourself.

Perhaps you are unconvinced. That's OK. This is a short book. Just give me a few minutes of your time, and an open mind.

My prayer is that by the time you finish reading, you will be so enamored of the beauty and power of these virtues that you will hunger for them, and long for the day when you can experience even a glimmer of any one of them in your daily life. These four virtues save lives and restore souls. You need them, and if you read, think, meditate and pray about them, you will discover that you really, really want them too.

Honesty

I will talk about honesty first because it offers four great gifts in the process of emotional healing.

First, honesty allows us to overcome denial.

Second, it helps us to uncover and name the empty places in our lives that we long to fill.

Third, honesty shines a light on the dark corners of our past and chases away the shadows of shame.

Fourth, shared honesty is an important step in developing compassion and a feeling of connection to the people around you.

As I explained in the introduction, emotional pain is a messenger that tells us that there are things missing in our lives—some virtues that we all deserved to grow up with but didn't. These might be love, security, respect, encouragement, tolerance, or any number of other essential virtues. We may be consciously aware of some of these missing virtues, but many others are invisible to us. It is difficult to name something you've never experienced, and yet the emotional pain of its absence is still tangibly real.

Honesty is the virtue we use to help us uncover what was missing.

The kind of honesty I'm referring to is not about not stealing (though that is important) nor is it the tactless honesty that encourages you to say hurtful things to others. It is, instead, a tool for self-discovery. It is the kind of honesty that allows you to see yourself accurately, acknowledge the things that have happened to you, and take responsibility for your own future.

I use the word honesty to represent a constellation of virtues that includes openness, truthfulness, and an ability to discern what is real and speak about it without shame. Honesty requires courage—first the courage to *look* at oneself without flinching, and second the courage to risk *being* oneself without reservation.

The first gift of honesty that we will explore is the gift of escaping from denial.

In order to heal what is missing in our lives, we must first acknowledge that our lives were not perfect; that there were important virtues that were not practiced or expressed in our families, and that we need to make an extra effort to acquire them now. This first step is called overcoming denial, and it requires that most fundamental of acts of honesty: opening our eyes.

The Power of Denial

Denial is not just an attempt to ignore those parts of our lives that we don't wish to acknowledge. Denial is the ability to *block from our conscious awareness* anything that we do not want to be able to see.

Humans are amazingly good at this.

Our ability to block our awareness of our personal challenges is so universal that it is even referred to by Jesus in one of his more amusing admonitions:

> *Why do you see the speck that is in your brother's eye, but do not notice the log that is in your own eye? How can you say to your brother, 'Brother, let me take out the speck that is in your eye,' when you yourself **do not see** the log that is in your own eye?*
> Luke 6:41-42

Note that He does not say that we are *ignoring* the log in our own eye, but that we *do not see* it. The log represents our personal challenges and unhealthy patterns. Admitting that we *might* have them is the first step in being able to see them.

The classic metaphor for denial is that of an elephant in a living room. The elephant is a problem, but everyone in the family is committed to *not* seeing it, as it eventually destroys the home. Some people in the family ignore the elephant, but some are *so good* at ignoring it that it really and truly disappears from their mind's eye.

The elephant can represent an alcoholic parent, mental illness, divorce, financial problems, unwanted pregnancy, sexual infidelity, addictions, *anything* that is a source of unresolved stress. And it doesn't matter how big the problem is, there will be some who are able to ignore it, and others who will blind themselves to its existence completely.

In order to co-exist with the elephant, each member of the family will develop his or her own coping mechanism, and these coping mechanisms will *also* either be invisible or accepted as rational behaviors, even though they are anything but.

As long as we continue to deny that both the elephant and the coping mechanisms exist, then they will continue to sabotage our lives. Once we acknowledge that there are aspects of our lives that we cannot even see, and which are completely irrational, then we can begin to look for their footprints.

This awakening, which is critical to any real emotional healing, gives us permission to ask for help in seeing the things that we have blocked from our awareness.

What are examples of things we might be in denial about?

We can be in denial about stressful experiences that have caused us pain; about the coping mechanisms we have developed to numb, distract, or hide this pain; about the problems caused by these coping mechanisms; and about the emotional pain itself. Some of the things we deny might hide in plain sight, while others may be truly blocked from our conscious memory and awareness.

We hide things in plain sight by justifying stressful or abusive behavior as normal. If our parents beat us, we might tell ourselves that "spare the rod, spoil the child" was proof that they loved us. A sexual assault by a friend or relative might be rewritten in our memories as a short-lived romance. A parent's alcoholism might be remembered as "daddy was sick a lot." Our mother's perfectionism and constant criticism might be justified as "she could do no wrong." The pain of living in crushing poverty might be brushed off with "it was a hard time for everyone." The death of a sibling might be minimized as "I hardly remember them anyway." We allow ourselves to remember these experiences, but we do not allow ourselves to remember the emotional pain they caused. We use rationalization and justifications to create a barrier between the two.

Other stressful experiences really are hidden from our memory. Some may have happened at a very young age. Others were so painful or traumatic that even though they were experienced later in life, we have blocked them from our memory because we don't have the tools we need to process them. While consciously forgotten, the emotional memory is still with us and can still cause us pain and shame. The four tools of healing will make it safer for these memories to surface.

Whether we remember our sources of stress and shame or not, we live with our coping mechanisms every day. One would think that this would make it harder to deny them, but deny them we do.

I'm not an alcoholic, I just like to have fun. I'm not a sex addict, I just have a strong libido. I'm not addicted to porn, I am just bored at night. I'm not obese, I have a condition. I'm not addicted to gambling, I'm just sure my luck is about to change.

Addictions are the way many people cope with the pain of early trauma and shame. They numb and distract us. By denying the addiction, we deny the pain that causes it. But addictions are not the only coping mechanisms available to us, therefore denial is not just about addiction, nor is it even only about big things. Denial is about our blindness to *any* unhealthy or irrational activity we engage in as a response to some trauma or shame.

Here is a teeny tiny example of one of my personal blind spots.

Something I was unaware of in my own behavior was my inability to close a drawer all the way. I invariably left drawers open one or two inches. This seems like a small thing, but I was completely unaware of it until my wife commented on it (in some exasperation). What I came to realize was that I resisted *completing* the act of closing drawers because I resisted *finishing* projects because a finished project could be judged as a *failure*, whereas an incomplete project couldn't. Dealing with my fear of judgment and failure helped me finish projects and, yes, close drawers. The point is not so much about *why* I didn't close drawers, but rather that I was completely *unaware* of the fact that I didn't.

My wife, on the other hand, noticed one day that she was saving used tubes of toothpaste for no apparent reason. When she allowed herself to become aware of this habit, she realized that a part of her was still expecting a time to come when we would be so impoverished that she would need the last spot of toothpaste in each of these tubes. That unconscious fear of scarcity was filling up our bathroom drawers! (The same ones I was leaving open two inches).

Going straight from "I'm willing to admit that I am in emotional pain and may need help" to admitting that we have an addiction or that we were abused or traumatized may be too big of a leap for many people. That is why it is OK to start by acknowledging *any* blind spot or coping mechanism. As soon as we are able to see even *one* small irrational behavior pattern that we've been blind to in the past, we open ourselves up to the possibility that there might be more. Open eyes. That's all you need to start.

Whether it is leaving drawers open or drinking too much alcohol, it is sobering to realize that the behaviors that we are blind to or try to deny are *not* invisible to the people around us. Just as it is easy to look at our friends and know if they drink, eat, spend, and gamble too much, or have affairs, scream at their kids, or beat their wives, the chances are that they know what you are doing too. The only ones who think otherwise are you and your loved ones who have agreed to live in denial too.

Living in denial does not reduce shame, it just makes it harder to heal. Remember, the point is not to figure out who is to blame for your pain. The point is to figure out what virtues you grew up missing so that you can develop them yourself. Denying that something was missing makes it impossible to fill that unmet need. Becoming aware of these little blind spots opens the door to healing by revealing the empty spaces we are trying to hide from ourselves.

Becoming aware of *our* blind spots also lets us feel compassion towards all of the other people we know whose behavior seems completely irrational to us. We can be more forgiving when we understand that people are not being irrational *on purpose*. I was not leaving drawers open in order to irritate my wife. I was leaving drawers open because I didn't realize what I was doing.

Being aware that we have blind spots and unconscious coping mechanisms also gives us a small measure of defense against those who would use them to manipulate us. Advertisers, politicians and cult leaders know that if they disguise their lies as the right kind of elephants, we will be unable to look straight at them.

"Daddy is not an alcoholic," for example, is such a big lie, that in order to survive in a family a child must be able to believe very big lies and never challenge authority. This makes lies like, "The world is ending in September," or "I am channeling the spirit of an alien priest from the planet Beta-Max," relatively easy to believe.

Likewise, when you are trying to explain some clear and obvious truth to someone and they just refuse to see it, know that there is probably some large family secret standing between them and your truth, blocking their view. They are not stupid, they are coping. Either that, or there is some large family secret standing between you and *their* truth. That's the thing about blind spots. You never *ever* know for *certain* which side of it you are standing on. So be tolerant, compassionate, and forgiving of others, and pray for clarity for yourself.

What does all of this have to do with honesty? The fact is that, whether you *ignore* the elephant in the living room, or *blind* yourself to it, you are never actually blind. Some part of you knows the truth.

In order to be honest with yourself, you don't actually need to know what the family secrets or personal challenges are that you are hiding from yourself. It can take years to figure all of that out. All you need to do is acknowledge the fact that you are in emotional pain and that emotional pain is a clear sign that there is *something* missing. When you admit that something is missing, you can begin the process of creating it for yourself.

Once this first step is taken, there are places you can go to learn how to become even more honest with yourself so you can uncover more information. We learn how to be honest by exploring our own experience, but we also learn through witnessing the honest sharing of other people.

If you really want to experience the "mother load" of open, honest, profound sharing, then you really are ready for the first step—the first step of twelve.

A Model of Honest Sharing

I've been trying to figure out a way to talk about this deep level of honesty that *doesn't* involve introducing you to a twelve-step program, but I can't. The two aspects of honesty that are most important for your personal growth—self-honesty and letting go of secrets—are best addressed through the unique strengths of an Anonymous meeting. So even if there are no twelve-step meetings in your town, and even if you refuse to even think about attending one yourself, let me illustrate some of the healing properties of honesty by describing what happens at one.

First of all, twelve-step meetings are created to serve the needs of people who have recognized that they might be missing something in their lives. Just showing up for a meeting requires a level of honesty and openness that is outside of most people's experience. "Closed" AA meetings are only for people who absolutely know that they have a problem with alcohol, but "open" AA meetings and most other kinds of meetings, such as Alanon, CoDA and dozens of others are open to anyone willing to consider the possibility that they might not be in complete control of their lives. If you have read this far in this book, then you would probably benefit from the right meeting.

When you walk into your first meeting, you may be carrying with you an entire backpack full of shame, fear, distrust, and resentment. It doesn't matter if you are at a meeting for alcoholics, sex addicts, over-eaters, co-dependents, or drug addicts, you will see all sorts of people from all walks of life. You may look around the room and think, "These people are crazy and they have no idea what I am going through. That guy is too rich, that guy is too poor, that guy is too old, that one is too young. None of them is dealing with the problems I have."

When the meeting starts, they will explain that everything said in the meeting stays in the meeting and is not to be repeated or referred to. It is a safe place to share secrets. You may be thinking, "Right. Like I'm going to tell these guys anything anyway."

They also explain that there is no "cross-talk," which means that after a person shares, no one else is allowed to comment, give advice or express judgment. Each person is to share from his or her *own* experience, and not express opinions about others' experience.

"What?" you may be thinking. "What is the point of listening to other people's problems if I'm not allowed to give them any useful advice?"

When the first person shares, they say, "Hi, my name is ___, and I'm (an alcoholic, sex addict, or whatever) and you may think, "Why would anyone say something like that?"

But everyone in the room smiles and says, "Hi ___," and it seems to give him or her comfort.

Then they tell a story about something awful they did this week, or some problem they are dealing with, or some mistake they made that they are trying to learn from, and you may think, "I can't believe someone would actually admit to this in public."

In most settings, this kind of honest sharing would generate a wave of discomfort in the people around them. Listeners would feel embarrassed for the person for being so open and vulnerable. They would look for an excuse to change the subject or remove themselves from the conversation. They might decide that the person sharing is a little weird or strange and avoid them in the future.

But this is not most settings. As you look around the room expecting to see frowns of disapproval and judgment on everyone's faces, you discover instead expressions of acceptance and connection. You see people nodding in understanding, and even maybe a few tears.

You are expecting shame and tension and fear to settle on the group, but it never does. It is like someone has thrown a stink bomb in the middle of the room, but the love and understanding of the people listening have turned it into perfume.

It makes no sense. When families talk about their problems or reveal secrets, the tension usually increases, but here it does just the opposite. As your own tension decreases, you listen more closely. Strangely, you start hearing a little bit of yourself in his story—maybe just a hint—a shared fear or a similar sense of humor.

Then a second person shares her story and something different rings true … and the next person's story, and the next. Pain is pain. Shame is shame. Longing is longing. The things that most people try to hold inside are even more universal than the things they are willing to share.

You may find yourself nodding in agreement along with others in the room. Those nods and that acceptance… maybe they could be for you too.

This sense of connection might not come with the first person who shares, or even in the first meeting. We have to experience a certain amount of honesty before we can develop an appreciation for it.

It may take time for our natural defenses to relax so that we can experience this kind of sharing as anything other than self-absorbed whining and complaint. It may take a while to calm our natural inclination to try to give advice and "fix" everyone else's problems. We may have to hear the stories and observe the progress before we begin to understand that the people sharing don't really need anyone's advice, let alone judgment. What they need is to take their

secrets and their shame out of the dark corners of their isolation and lay them out where sunshine and fresh air can
put them in perspective and blow the stink off of them.

Keeping our problems to ourselves makes us feel alone,
which increases our desire to participate in inappropriate
behaviors. Isolating ourselves allows us to believe that we
are the only people in the world struggling with our problems. Keeping secrets allows us to believe that *our* problems,
our mistakes, *our* patterns are so bad that they will never be
accepted or forgiven.

When we listen to and share stories, we realize that we
are *not* alone, we are *not* the only ones dealing with these
issues, and, no matter what we have done, we can receive
forgiveness and learn to forgive ourselves. Looking around
the room, we see people who have made terrible mistakes,
done destructive things and are struggling to deal with the
consequences. Yet, when we look at them, what we learn to
see is the nobility of the struggle.

Over time, the mistakes that people have made in the
past become less important than the progress they are currently making. We are inspired by their growth. We are attracted to their perseverance. We begin to recognize virtues
in them that we don't even have names for. In short, we
begin to love them. We have no desire to condemn them,
and we can't imagine a loving God condemning them either. If we can forgive them, and God can forgive them, then
we can begin to imagine the possibility of being forgiven
ourselves.

As I said, all of this sense of connection and acceptance
will not magically descend upon you at your first meeting.
It will take time, and, just as importantly, it will take an attitude of openness to the unknown. I hope you give it a try
because I don't know of any other setting that even comes
close to creating the healing atmosphere of the recovery community.

If you are unable or unwilling to try a twelve-step meeting, then keep in mind the essential requirements: safety, honesty, acceptance, mutual sharing, no advice. If you can find a group of friends or a support group to offer you these things, then go for it. It can work if everyone present understands what you are attempting and why.

Seeing a therapist is not the same. While there are some things a professional therapist can do better than a twelve-step group, therapists don't share their stories. Therapists are paid to be accepting. Therapists often like to give advice. Therapists charge by the hour.

Going to a meeting four to eight times a week for your first few months of personal work will give you the added advantage of hearing hundreds of stories and receiving thousands of nods of acceptance.

Now that I have described a meeting, and have, I hope, piqued your interest, let's take a look at what kinds of things it is valuable to share in this kind of safe setting. What are we being honest about, what are we disclosing, and what are we hoping to gain by the process?

❀

Why We Self-Disclose

If we want to change our unhealthy, irrational behavior, then we will have to discover its roots. What is causing the shame that drives us to our unhealthy, numbing behaviors? What are we hiding from ourselves? What have we forgotten?

In the recovery community, there is a saying that goes

"The pain of remembering can't be any worse than the pain of *knowing* and yet not remembering."

Read that line again. It is important.

If we weren't in pain, we would not be engaging in numbing behavior.

If we had *truly* forgotten, if we did not carry an *inner knowing* of the source of our pain, then we would not be in pain. It would not have any power over us and our choices.

If some part of us knows why we are in pain, then, by removing one layer of numbing shame at a time, we can eventually figure it out.

We do that by shining a light on our feelings and behaviors, removing the shame, then looking beneath those behaviors to find the hidden motivation. We do this over and over again, one layer at a time by sharing our feelings and experiences with others. Sometimes, sharing will blow a little bit of dust off of our pasts. Other times it will dig deep enough to unearth skeletons.

The process of sharing is a way to call ourselves to account. So why does it need to be so public? Why can't we lie in bed and think about things that have happened to us and explore our feelings in the privacy of our homes using internal consultation?*

There are several reasons.

When we start to share with a group, things come out of our mouths that we didn't expect to say or know that we knew. Having witnesses solidifies the sharing and makes it real

Self-disclosure is a way of shining a light on the shadows of our lives. When we remember painful things, we often take more responsibility for them than we should. Having witnesses who show empathy helps put what happened to us in perspective.

Honest self-disclosure that is followed by acceptance rather than judgment helps remove shame. When we remem-

---

*A meditation technique discussed in *The Secret of Emotions*.

ber shameful experiences, we often exaggerate their importance, making ourselves feel even more evil and shameful. Witnesses who are not shocked or appalled remind us that making mistakes does not make us evil.

Humans are social creatures. We discover ourselves through our interactions with others. We learn, not just from our own sharing, but by listening to the sharing of others.

Our understanding of our identity becomes clearer and more concrete when it is reflected in the responses of those who truly see us. Acknowledgment is a form of identity confirmation. Self-disclosure is a tool for integration of all parts of our personality and all past experiences into one coherent identity. When you share different aspects of your life with the same people over the course of months or years, they don't experience you as a collection of isolated stories. They don't see a parent, an employee, a religious person or a person who is struggling. They see a single, complex human. Their ability to accept that complexity makes it easier for you to integrate the different ways that you see yourself.

In addition to being a tool for self-discovery, honest self-disclosure is a form of profound sharing, which makes it an amazing creative process. Sharing is one of the ways that humans reflect the generative power of the Creator. It transfers knowledge or experience from one soul to another—effectively doubling its potential—at no material cost. By sharing experience, strength and hope, the amount of experience, strength and hope in the world is multiplied many fold.

As George Bernard Shaw said: "If you have an apple and I have an apple and we exchange these apples then you and I will still each have one apple. But if you have an idea and I have an idea and we exchange these ideas, then each of us will have two ideas."

The wisdom that is expressed in some of these meetings is staggering. The thought that that wisdom is now multiplying exponentially as it is internalized and then shared by others is one of the things that gives me hope for the human race. The belief that this wisdom can eventually heal the planet is why I'm writing this book.

What Self-Disclosure *Isn't*

It is important to make a distinction between therapeutic self-disclosure and confession—or such unhelpful, even potentially destructive behaviors as complaining, blaming, back-biting or self-flagellation.

First of all, we are not asking anyone to forgive us, give us penance, or tell us that what we did was acceptable. The people to whom we disclose are not stand-ins for God. They are simply witnesses. They help lock what comes out of our mouths into objective reality so that we can remember it and have it reflected back to us through other people's eyes.

The purpose is not to complain, blame or back-bite. The focus is not on what others may have done to us, but what we felt and internalized as a result of it. The experiences we relate are not *true* in the absolute sense. They are simply true for *us*. To the best of our ability, we do not reveal incriminating details about other people's behavior. We speak in "I" sentences.

The purpose is not to beat ourselves up for what we have done, but to shine a light on it so that we can understand our own hidden motivations and reactions. One of the paradoxical benefits of this type of honesty is that as we *increase* our sense of personal responsibility, we *reduce* toxic shame.

⚭

What We Self-Disclose

Whether it is in a meeting or in our daily lives, we should have a goal of being able to honestly share our feelings, our thoughts, opinions and observations, our experiences, and our positive regard for others. To the degree that these topics relate to our personal lives (rather than politics or gossip) they are also appropriate to share in a meeting.

Appropriate topics include:

Experiences that caused intense emotions that we might need assistance to identify and resolve. When we have strong sensations—good, bad or ugly—it means that *something* is going on with us. Talking them out can help us understand and identify what it is.

Experiences that we learned from. When we start paying attention to what goes on in the background of our lives, it seems as though every day brings a new flash of awareness. Journaling is a wonderful way to keep track of these insights, but there is a real joy and sense of empowerment that comes from being able to share these with people who care about your growth.

Experiences that we would like assistance in solving, resolving, interpreting or understanding. It might seem counterproductive to expect help from a group that is committed to not giving advice to one another, yet help does indeed come. First, the voicing of the dilemma often draws forth from our own well of wisdom the insight that we need. Second, while others won't tell you what *you* should do, they can share, using "I" statements, what *they* have experienced in vaguely similar situations. This might seem like a game of semantics, but the difference is very real. Advice invites either resistance or compliance. Parallel experiences invite exploration and contemplation.

Experiences that we simply need to have acknowledged as true, valuable or real. Sometimes all we need is to say "this happened to me" and have others sit in witness.

Sometimes the experience that we most need to share with others is the experience of sitting in silent, supportive witness to the other people in the room. Listening, in this situation, is not a passive activity. It is an active gift to the ones being heard—sometimes for the first time in their entire lives.

My friend Phyllis Peterson, author of **Remaining Faithful**, tells me her long road to recovery was dependent upon external validation. She attended a twelve-step program for recovery from incest during which the pain of her inner child within was witnessed and validated over and over again by the compassionate listeners of the group. Through this process, the toxic shame and guilt she felt was finally transferred to her abuser. Without this external validation, she would have been unable to eventually develop the skill of internal consultation.

Letting Go of Secrets

Some of the most important self-disclosure involves letting go of secrets—personal secrets and family secrets. This is incredibly frightening. When I tell people this, they often protest—sometimes quite angrily—or even get up and leave the room.

Before you throw this book in the trash, let me clarify that secrets should only be shared in a safe setting. There are, however, several reasons why it is worth the effort to find or create such a setting for yourself—either in a twelve-step group or in private therapy.

It takes energy to keep a secret

Take a moment to consider the physical, emotional and mental cost of keeping secrets. The longer we keep one, the more energy it takes to keep it hidden—energy that is then not available for all of the other wonderful, creative things you could be doing with your life. The lifetime cost of just one big family secret might be enough for someone to have accomplished great things *if* they'd been able to use that energy constructively instead.

For example, I had three great secrets as a young child:

1) My father had left us,

2) The reason for his abandonment (in my mind) was that there was something profoundly wrong with me, and

3) The proof that I was defective (in my mind) was that I wet the bed.

These three secrets took enormous amounts of energy to keep hidden. Like all children, I still saw the world as a mysterious place. One of my beliefs was that adults—and especially women—could read my mind. After all, my mother knew when I had done something wrong, no matter how little evidence there was. Consequently, I was sure that every adult I met would be able to see right through my soul and know that I was flawed.

To prevent that, I tried to keep my thoughts from drifting towards the sources of my shame. That was about as effective as not thinking about pink elephants. It affected my ability to concentrate in school, my willingness to make friends, and my creativity, because part of my mental energy was always elsewhere, trying to block thoughts of how broken I was.

All of us have secrets. We have parts of our identity that we are ashamed of. Though most of us no longer believe that others can read our minds, we nevertheless devote an incredible amount of mental energy to trying to hide the subtle clues that might let someone else guess what we don't want them to know. Just think of the wasted energy!

Secrets hold us hostage.
Secrets can stop us from doing things we want to do for fear of exposure. For example, when I was in High School, I was so poor that I did not own a suit or a tie, and since I had no father or male family members, I didn't have anyone to borrow them from without revealing how poor I was. When my Graphic Arts Club took its annual field trip to a nearby city, dinner at a fancy restaurant was included as a treat. The only problem was that we were required to wear a jacket and tie. Rather than admit my situation to my fellow students, I simply didn't go. The teacher and students all thought that I was being a snob and didn't want to be seen with them, when the exact opposite was true.

How often do we subtly rearrange our lives so that we won't have to admit to our little family secrets?

Secrets blackmail us.

Shame can make you feel that you do not deserve success, but secrets can make you afraid to achieve success because you fear the scrutiny that comes with it. This subtle self-blackmail is more than just not doing something that might reveal a specific secret; it is avoiding doing *anything* that might draw attention to yourself. When we have big secrets, we are like families in protective custody. We are hiding who we really are, and trying to keep a low profile. This means we can't afford to excel in anything. We certainly can't go into politics, but even applying for jobs that do background checks or call references or check credit scores can send us into hiding. Acting, public speaking, making a lot of money, starting a business, traveling abroad, anything that would make someone—especially someone in authority—look at us closely provokes a fear that someone will figure out what our fatal flaw might. This background paranoia can keep us from giving life our best shot and reaching for our dreams.

Secrets disrupt honest interactions.

Many of us have more than passive secrets. We may be struggling with active addictions, fears, personality disorders, emotional pain and other issues that require conscious effort to keep under control when we're in social situations. I picture these personal issues as invisible monkeys that sit on our shoulders—poking, prodding, pulling our hair and screeching in our ears while we are trying to hold "normal" conversations with "normal" people. We can neither speak honestly nor listen objectively to what others are saying when our secrets are constantly threatening to highjack our conversations.

Secrets are not so secret.

If all of these reasons for letting go of secrets have not convinced you that should find a way to be more open with people, then you are really not going to like this last reason. The simple fact is, that many of our most closely held secrets are not really very secret to the people we work with or even meet on the street. Those invisible monkeys that are screeching in our ears are often not so invisible—or silent— to others. To some degree or another, most of us are consciously aware of other people's blind spots as well as their supposed secrets. Like the abused spouse who tries to cover bruises with layers of makeup, we think that we are fooling people, but we aren't. To an even greater degree, we are often *subconsciously* aware of other people's issues because our hearts perceive what our minds try to hide. We notice the empty spaces in conversations, hear the tension in each other's voices, catch the nervous glances, read between the lines.

All of us subconsciously respond to each other's inner reality, secret or not. Usually our conscious and unconscious awareness of each other's secrets is papered over by small talk and polite redirection. Sometimes, however, people's secrets clash. Our "invisible monkeys" are not so invisible to each other. When angry secrets, guilty secrets and fearful secrets collide, all hell can break loose. One person's invisible "alcoholic monkey" for example may be secretly attacking someone else's "victim monkey," leading communication in completely unpredictable and unproductive directions. Workplace dynamics are often dominated by this kind of covert war of secrets, with the primary weapon being the threat of exposure. Sometimes I wonder how we ever get anything done at all.

The fewer secrets we keep, the less power they have over us. But secrets don't just disappear on their own. They must be transformed from *secret* to *known* and *accepted*. While I am certainly not advocating publicly sharing your secrets over the water cooler, it is important to know what your secrets are and to share them with *someone* so that these secrets can begin to lose their mystery and their power. By sharing them with *someone*, you can gain an objective appreciation for how few of them really need to stay secret after all.

Becoming Whole

If keeping secrets from others robs us of a portion of our energy, then keeping secrets from ourselves robs us of a part of ourselves. It is amazing how much we can hide behind one secret and never let ourselves see.

My secret about wetting the bed, for example, was so shameful for me that I simply refused to think about it. Years later, in college, I would still mentally look away whenever the thought of it came up—until one day when I finally asked myself, "Why don't I like myself?"

What I discovered was a whole rat's nest of beliefs and attitudes hiding behind the skeleton in that closet. I believed that bed-wetting was a psychological and moral problem rather than simply the result of a slowly developing bladder. It was the proof that my sisters used in order to convince me that there was something wrong with me and that I should be shipped off to some institution for defective children. I seriously lived in fear that someday men in white coats would come and take me away (ha ha, hee hee, ho ho). Such ideas are laughable to an adult, but the adult me had never given himself permission to look at the problem. It had been locked away in the secret closet since well before a rational perspective could take a look at it.

Shining a light on that secret allowed me to integrate my childhood fears with my adult understanding. Without that integration, my childhood fear of being defective would continue to subconsciously affect my decisions and influence my relationships.

Many people's deep, dark secrets turn out to be quite innocent and simple once they see the light of day. But they will never know this is true if they refuse to take a look.

As I've said, I am not advocating walking up to complete strangers and telling them all of your darkest secrets. The point is to find a safe time and place to let go of your secrets so that they no longer hold you hostage. This is a situation in which starting with a single, private therapist might be easier than sharing with a large group. On the other hand, sharing with a group can shine a lot of light into your life all at once and air out a lot of fear and shame.

It is important to remember that self disclosure is not an end unto itself. It has a purpose, a goal. Some of the goals I've mentioned are: exposing your heart to the beauty of honesty, reducing shame, creating connections that can generate compassion, self-discovery and integration through self-disclosure, and reclaiming the wasted energy that it takes to hide secrets from yourself and others.

The result of all of these goals is an increased ability to be fully present; to be able to bring all of yourself—past and present, strengths and weaknesses—to every situation you enter. If we have secrets; if we are overwhelmed by shame, then we can't be fully present or feel fully accepted. The cumulative effect of being dishonest with ourselves—by constantly hiding who we really are and pretending that we are someone different—is that we end up living someone else's life.

We deserve better than that.

Forgiveness

Honesty helps us learn about ourselves and heal our shame. It also is an important part of forgiving ourselves, which, in turn, also helps us heal shame. Forgiving others helps us heal our anger and create more serenity in our lives. Reducing the level of anger in the world as a whole may do more than anything else to improve the quality of everyone's lives.

There is a well-known saying that holding onto resentment is like drinking poison and waiting for the other person to die. Resentment poisons our soul, but before we can let go of it, we need to understand the relationship between forgiveness, anger, resentment and injustice.

♦ **Forgiveness is a willingness to acknowledge anger, but let go of resentment.**

♦ **Anger is a healthy emotional response to a perceived injustice.**

♦ **Resentment is an unhealthy emotional investment in a *past* injustice.**

To invest in something is to store something of value in it for future use. When we invest our emotions in a past injustice, we have committed our energy to a particular outcome or response. Until we achieve that outcome, our emotional energy sits and festers instead of being used for something positive, productive, and in the *present*. When that outcome is unhealthy, inappropriate, unachievable or out-side of our control, then we may cut ourselves off from that emotional energy forever.

Forgiveness releases this emotional energy so that it can be used positively. This frees us to experience *other* emotions and perceive the *presence* of virtues in our lives rather than focusing on the absence of justice.

Guilt, shame and anger stand between us and our ability to accept the virtues and positive emotions that are missing in our lives. Guilt and shame convince us that we still don't deserve them. Anger tells us that it is still someone else's responsibility to give them to us.

Many of us carry so much resentment that we *didn't* receive the positive treatment that we deserved, that we are oblivious to the fact that we can give *ourselves* the spiritual gifts that we need *today*. Forgiving ourselves and others opens up our capacity to receive these blessings.

- ♦ Forgiving others helps us heal our relationships
- ♦ Forgiving others helps us let go of our victim mentality.
- ♦ Forgiving others helps free us from the past.
- ♦ Forgiving ourselves helps us heal our shame.
- ♦ Forgiving ourselves involves letting go of our feelings of guilt—for who we are and for what we've done.
- ♦ Forgiving ourselves makes it safe to admit our mistakes.
- ♦ Admitting our mistakes makes it easier to make amends …which makes it easier to forgive ourselves.

Forgiving both ourselves and others for the mistakes we've all made makes it easier to let go of old beliefs and explore new ones.

Why *Not* Forgive?

With all of these wonderful reasons to practice forgiveness, why do so many people resist? I believe that most of the reasons why people are afraid to forgive are based on mistaken ideas of what forgiveness really is. Forgiving is not forgetting. It does not give people permission to commit additional injustices. It is not being a patsy, wimp or coward.

Forgiveness does not let people off the hook. It only lets them off of *your* hook. People will still suffer the natural consequences of their own actions, it is just that you won't be keeping score. Will they "get away with it?" No. Their unjust action will follow them around for the rest of their lives and beyond. Don't let it do the same for you.

Some people believe that holding onto anger is a way to punish the person who hurt them, so they hold onto it as a form of revenge. Of course, anger hurts the person feeling the anger more than the one they are angry at, so it kind of backfires. Buddha is claimed to have said that holding onto anger is like picking up a hot coal with the intention of throwing it at someone else. You are the one who gets burned.

Holding onto anger until someone apologizes is equally counterproductive. The anger creates tension; the tension creates distance; the distance makes it harder for the other person to apologize and increases the likelihood that they will find a way to feel as though *they* are the injured party.

Forgiveness is not reconciliation, which involves re-establishing a harmonious relationship with the person who hurt you. Sometimes reconciliation is appropriate, but it takes two people and a safe situation. Sometimes we have to forgive from a distance, and even forgive people who still hate us and want to hurt us. That's their Karma. Ours is to let it go and move on to something better and brighter.

If we *fear* reconciliation, we have a right to listen to that fear, but we shouldn't let that get in the way of forgiveness.

If we *long for* reconciliation, we have a right to feel that longing, but we would be wise to direct it towards a relationship that is worthy of our longing.

For example, our parents represented God to us when we were infants, and no matter how badly they treated us, we still long to reconcile with them because we spiritually want to reconcile with God. Fortunately, we don't need our parents' cooperation to do that. We can bypass the human symbols of God and express our longing towards the virtues that a loving God has blessed us with. Forgiveness is a good one to start with.

Apologies, punishment, forgetting, reconciliation— these are all specific outcomes that we may cling to through our resentment. Since they are all outside of our control, clinging to them may leave us swimming in resentment for decades. Letting go of these expectations will free our energies for more productive pursuits.

The Stages of Anger

There is a school of thought that says that the secret of forgiveness is to never judge other people's actions as inappropriate so that you never get angry in the first place.

If you will forgive my French, I think that is bull shit.

Emotions are messengers. Ignoring them or slamming the door in their face will not make them go away.

Anger is an emotional response to the absence of justice. Justice is *very* important, and there is very little of it in the world today. That makes anger very important. Ignoring injustice will not make it go away, and will not give us the opportunity to correct it.

Being able to **feel** anger, **recognize** its source, **confirm** its validity, **identify** the injustice that is being perpetrated, make wise choices as to how to **respond** effectively, and then take positive **action** are among the most important thing we can do as humans.

Let me put that in a bulleted list so you can find it later:

- ◆ Feel the Anger
- ◆ Recognize its Source
  (this is an emotional process)
- ◆ Confirm its Validity
  (your right to have emotions)
- ◆ Identify the specific Injustice
  (this is a rational process)
- ◆ Choose an appropriate Response
- ◆ Take positive Action

When anger is allowed to follow its natural course, it only lasts a few minutes and results in positive corrective action, even if that corrective action is nothing more than a smile and a friendly, "That's OK. I don't mind."

When your perception of an injustice is *not* allowed to take its natural course, then it gets blocked and the energy of anger builds instead of being released through action. When anger lingers, it can turn into resentment or rage. That is when it stops being healthy and starts being dangerous.

Anger's natural progression can be blocked at any point along the way. Perhaps you are trying not to **feel** anger; you are having a difficult time **recognizing** its source; the **validity** of your feeling is being denied, you can't identify the specific **injustice** you are responding to; you are either having a difficult time finding an appropriate **response**, or you are emotionally attached to an inappropriate response; and/or you are unable to **act** on the response you have chosen.

Practicing forgiveness, then, is not simply about ignoring injustice or letting go of anger, it is removing the internal blocks to anger's natural progression—one step at a time—so that the anger can serve its purpose and walk away, leaving you feeling informed, respected and empowered.

Feeling Anger

The first step in forgiving is allowing yourself to get angry.

Anger, remember, is a messenger. It tells us when we have experienced an injustice.

If we try to forgive before we listen to the message, the messenger will not go away. It will just go into hiding.

If we try to forgive before we listen to the messenger, we are ignoring the injustice—we are saying that the injustice was not real, it did not matter, or that it was not really an injustice at all.

This is really the same as saying that *we deserved it.*

You see, anger is an automatic sensation, like wrinkling your nose when you smell something bad. You can't choose to *not* sense it, you can only choose to acknowledge it or ignore it. If you ignore the sensation—if you pretend not to smell anything foul—then what you are telling yourself is that nothing unfair happened; that stinky is really sweet.

In order to perceive the unjust as just, and for the foul to seem fair, you must convince yourself that you deserved whatever unfair treatment you received. You are, in essence, saying, "The way I've been treated isn't so bad after all; this is normal; I deserve it; I can live with this stench for the rest of my life."

Believing that you deserved whatever bad things were said to you—or done to you—makes you feel unlovable, unworthy, dirty, or sinful. This is not healthy. We can't hold these beliefs about ourselves and still feel full of life, love and energy. Negative self-talk, even if it is completely unconscious, drains us of hope and enthusiasm. It makes us small. It weakens us.

In other words, when we deny that we have been treated unfairly so that we can avoid acknowledging anger, we are telling ourselves that we deserve to be treated poorly. If we believe that we deserved to be treated badly in the past, then we will also believe that we deserve to be treated badly in the future.

Because of this belief, we will do things that are self-destructive, like start relationships with unhealthy or abusive people, or engage in compulsive behaviors.

This is why processing anger and learning forgiveness is one of the four tools of healing. It is not just about letting go of resentment, it is about releasing the depression and self-loathing that is sitting on top of the resentment, trying to keep the anger in check.

Why Not Feel Angry?

If anger is a natural and healthy response to injustice, why are so many people afraid to acknowledge their anger? Here are just a few reasons:

♦ They fear that anger will spill over into rage or violence.
♦ They fear anger will fester into resentments that will keep them focused on the bad that has happened in their lives.
♦ They fear that anger and resentment will cut them off from the people they love, who may have unintentionally treated them unjustly.
♦ They fear that if they show their anger, the people who hurt them will respond with anger and hurt them even more.
♦ They have been told that "good" people don't get angry.
♦ They fear getting angry at the people in authority in their lives—especially those who represented God—for fear it will cut them off from salvation.
♦ They fear "rocking the boat" and attracting disapproval.
♦ They fear damaging their family's reputation.

All of these fears are perfectly reasonable if you haven't learned how to work through your anger to find forgiveness and serenity. It is prudent to not start a process that you don't know how to finish. Allowing yourself to feel anger with no end in sight can have dire physical, emotional and social consequences. Fortunately, that is not what I am asking you to do. Go ahead; hold your anger in for just a little while longer. Let me walk you through the steps that will get you all the way to the other side. Knowing all of the steps that are in front of you makes it less likely that you will get stuck when the emotion of anger tries to overwhelm you. When you can see where you are going, you will know in your heart that you can control the anger rather than letting it control you.

The next steps, after giving yourself permission to feel anger, are to recognize the source, validate the anger and identify the specific injustice. Since recognizing the source and identifying the specifics are closely related, I will discuss both of them after explaining the importance of validating our emotional perceptions.

Validating Anger

When we hear voices, we instinctively look around to see who is speaking. If we can't find anyone, then we begin to doubt our sanity.

When we feel angry, we instinctively review our situation to see if we are being treated unfairly or unjustly. If we can't find a source for our feelings, then we, again, begin to doubt our sanity. That is why most of us will do whatever it takes to identify some source of irritation to justify our anger.

After identifying a possible source of our emotion, our next step is to mentally *confirm or validate* the spiritual perception. Our mind asks "do I see evidence of an injustice?"

Anger, by its nature, is a kind of accusation. When we feel anger, we are saying "someone or something here is not fair." This attitude of accusation sets us up for resistance— both internal and external. If we are angry at a person, they are likely to say, "Hey, wait a minute! I didn't do anything wrong." If we are angry at a person we love or fear, we don't even need *them* to argue with us, we argue with ourselves. Part of us wants to defend or justify their actions so that our anger does not hurt or anger *them*, while another part of us needs to acknowledge *our* hurt and anger.

Even if all we are angry at is a *situation*, one part of us will be thinking "This is not fair!" while a contrary voice inside our head says, "It is not the world's fault. If something bad has happened to you, you must have deserved it!"

This sets up a tug-of-war between our emotional perceptions and our mental need to validate what we feel. We try to pull the world, the other person, or even ourselves towards one perception of reality, while they try to pull us back towards another.

Until these dueling realities are resolved; until we can mentally validate our perceptions, it is impossible for us to formulate a reasonable and rational response to the situation. And until we do, we are stuck feeling angry, and rational action is almost impossible.

How long can we stay in this emotional limbo—angry, but not quite sure if we have a right to be?

An entire lifetime.

Just listen to people.

Anyone who feels the need to explain *why* they are angry is in the process of trying to convince themselves that they have a right to be. Once our head and our heart are in agreement, there is no longer any need to talk about it. It is time to move on to action.

So how do we escape this tug of war?

By letting go.

If we keep pulling, our anger will keep us emotionally bound to this situation forever. We can't convince them they are guilty and they can't convince us they are innocent.

If we stop pulling but don't let go, we get dragged into the opposing perception. We are accepting their innocence. In doing so, are pretending that the situation was not really unjust at all; that we had no valid reason to be angry. We are denying our reality and saying that we deserve to be treated badly. This will just lead to depression.

When we let go, we stop trying to convince the other person (or our inner voice) that we are right. We look for a *different* kind of validation that our feelings are legitimate.

When our conflict is with another person, this can be as simple as saying to ourselves, "I do not need them to agree with me on this. I can allow myself to feel slighted by this situation even if they don't think I have a reason to. They don't have to understand my perspective." Since we ultimately have absolutely no control over other people's thoughts or feelings, letting go of the need to convince them that *our* feelings are valid is the only rational path to serenity. It allows us to validate our own feelings, and prepare to respond.

When our conflict is bigger than one person or is left over from childhood trauma, then self-validation may not be enough. When we are having a tug-of-war with God, the Universe, or our own inner demons, then telling ourselves that we are right won't end the argument. These internal conflicts often involve deep, painful injustices that have never moved from anger to response because the anger was never acknowledged as legitimate. Our fingers are gripping the rope so tightly that we are afraid to let go.

In these cases, we need someone to hold onto the rope for us while we let go—someone standing on our side in the tug-of-war to let us know that if we let go, we won't be alone in our perceptions. We need someone to stand witness to the injustices we have experienced.

What does that look like?

It looks like open, honest sharing. Find a trusted friend or therapist to whom you can describe the situation in private. Tell them that you don't want advice, just confirmation that what you are perceiving is valid. Before you can *let go* of anger, you first need to hear someone say, "that sounds awful. That was really unfair. You have a *right* to be angry."

Once you are reassured that your feelings can be trusted, only then is it safe to let them go and begin to formulate an appropriate response to their message.

Note: you need to hear that your anger is valid *even if it isn't true*. You can't see a situation clearly until the fog of anger clears, and the fog of anger will not clear as long as it is being argued with, dismissed or minimized. While this might seem dishonest, what we are really doing at this stage is validating our *right* to have our emotional response. We will address the validity of our *reason* for feeling angry later.

Arguing over the *reason* for our anger before establishing our *right* to feel angry is why small fights can escalate so easily. When both people are wrong, neither is able to see their part in the problem until the other person's wrongs are acknowledged first. It is not so much about making the other person wrong as it is about legitimizing our own experience of reality.

The most terrifying thing in the world is to fear that you can't trust your own perception of reality. It is like hearing voices without being able to find the speaker. Feeling anger and being told that you have no reason to makes you feel crazy. The fear that you might be both wrong and crazy makes you work even harder to prove that you do have a reason. Once someone else validates that you do have a *right* to be upset, then the fear dissipates and you can consider your reason more dispassionately. Then your desire for connection, understanding, compassion and forgiveness can take over.

Once fear and anger are not clouding our judgment, we can find a rational and appropriate response to whatever situation it was that we felt was unjust.

Often, once fear and anger, guilt and depression are not clouding our judgment, we immediately realize that the most rational and appropriate response... is to forgive.

What We Are Angry About

With so much injustice in the world, we have a lot to be angry about. However, it helps to make a distinction between the deeper sources of our anger and the specific injustices that trigger our day-to-day flashes of irritation. In a way, our life-long feelings of having been mistreated, abandoned, misunderstood, abused and all the rest are like red-hot coals just under the surface of our awareness, while the individual events that trigger our awareness of that anger are like drops of gasoline that make a bright light, but are not the real source of the heat.

When you read those words, "mistreated, abandoned, misunderstood and abused," some of you thought, "Yeah, that's right," while others thought, "Come now, aren't you being a bit melodramatic?"

Not at all.

We live in a culture whose underlying beliefs—religious, scientific and psychological—are that humans are fundamentally sinful, violent, competitive and in need of fixing, when in reality, humans are glorious, noble reflections of God in need of education and guidance. That disconnect between our reality and the way the world sees us is so unjust and unfair that it is enough to make anyone who feels it very, very angry, or very, very sad.

Both the deep-seated injustices and the day-to-day slights need to be validated so they can be resolved, but the nature of the resolution is somewhat different. Deep-seated injustices are often very old, and the range of appropriate healthy responses may be very narrow. If resentment is an emotional investment in a specific outcome, then it is important that we choose an outcome that is within our control. Deep-seated injustices changed our beliefs about ourselves, so a healthy response must be more about transforming those beliefs than changing someone else.

Specific injustices can be approached on a more pragmatic level, with a much wider range of appropriate choices and actions. We will work through what some of those might be shortly, but let's start by looking at some of the deeper reasons why we are angry—starting with why we are angry with ourselves. Exploring why we are angry with ourselves and the things we think we might need to be forgiven for will give us a pretty good idea of what our core sources of anger are. When we move on to forgiving others, we will have a better idea of what it is they might need forgiveness for.

Once we appreciate our core sources of anger, it will be easier to separate them from our day-to-day sources of irritation. That way we don't end up fighting life-long battles every time something upsets us, and it will be easier to choose an appropriate response.

Forgiving Ourselves

Feeling angry with ourselves, feeling guilt and feeling shame are not the same, but they are close siblings. Healing one will help heal the others.

John Bradshaw, the author of **Healing the Shame That Binds You**, says that the difference between healthy shame and toxic shame is that with healthy shame, you know you've *made* a mistake. With toxic shame, you believe that you *are* the mistake.

We could say something similar about *feeling* guilty and *being* guilty. We feel guilty when we commit a sin—that is we do something that we know in advance is hurtful to ourselves or others. We *are* guilty when we feel that we *are* the sin—that our very existence is a stain on the world, and there is nothing we can do to change that.

Shame tells us that we are a mistake and must change who we are to be acceptable. Guilt tells us that we are sinful—that we have committed an unforgivable injustice—and we must be punished before we will be acceptable.

The way we punish ourselves is to refuse to forgive ourselves. We commit to remaining angry with ourselves—even when we have no idea of what it is we have done wrong, or why it is we *are* wrong.

As children, many of us felt this sense of "wrongness" and tried to make sense of it. We created elaborate explanations as to what our sins might be. Just because we can't remember what those explanations were doesn't mean that we don't still believe them. Until we forgive them, we will continue to live in anticipation of an unspecified punishment every single day.

So the big question is, what do we believe that we are guilty of? What kinds of things must we be telling ourselves in order to justify carrying around this burden of unforgiven guilt?

For those of us who live with guilt and anger, we have a conscious awareness of many little sins that we are guilty of, but these often just serve to hide a bigger sin from our awareness. For example, we use all of the people we've hurt in relationships as an explanation of why we are so evil, rather than asking ourselves why we are afraid to commit to a relationship in the first place. If we can find a way to name these big sins, then we shine a light on them. When we do that, we usually discover that they are either something that we have made up, they are misunderstandings, or they are exaggerated. Naming the "sins" that we have been hiding from ourselves for years often exposes them as laughable.

As children, we believe ourselves to be the center of the universe, so in our attempts to make sense of the confusing events of our lives, we take responsibility for everything that goes wrong.

I don't know what you feel guilt for, but I felt guilty for: being born (original sin and all of that stuff), being born a male, wetting the bed, causing my parent's divorce, letting my sister be sent away to a children's home when I was obviously the one who was defective, allowing women to fall in love with me knowing I would break their hearts because I was defective and unable to meet their needs, and for taking up space on the planet when there were so many more worthy souls who deserved my place.

On top of these major sins, I added a daily list of every failure to anticipate the needs and expectations of the women around me—because they were proof positive of my biggest sin of all: I didn't love and care for other people enough to earn my place in the world. Life was not a gift, it was a debt, and I was failing to make my daily payments. I was guilty, and I couldn't forgive myself.

All of these "sins" seem funny to me, now that I have given them a name. They are absurd. No sane person would believe them. Yet I can assure you that these, and many more just like them, rattle around in the heads of most people. If they *didn't*, then most people would behave much differently than they do. Consider, for example, the popularity of such songs as **Highway to Hell**, and **Bad to the Bone,** or video games such as **Grand Theft Auto**. These were created for people who have given up on believing that they are forgivable.

If people liked themselves; if people forgave themselves for their imperfections, then people would treat themselves (and each other) with more kindness and respect.

Forgiving a Belief

In **The Secret of Emotions,** I described an exercise called "internal consultation" in which you try to get in touch with inner emotions and sensations. This same technique can help you get in touch with the beliefs behind your feelings of guilt and anger, and create an opportunity for forgiveness.

In my original description of internal consultation, we started with physical sensations and tried to get in touch with emotional sensations that were hiding in the background. In this brief review of the exercise, you will start with sensations relating to guilt or anger at yourself and try to walk it backwards to find the underlying beliefs or events that triggered them. While this exercise can be done alone, it may bring up some deep emotions, memories and questions. Having a professional therapist to help you sort out your feelings and mirror your experience can be very helpful.

Emotions have sensations associated with them. Guilt, shame and anger all have a slightly different "flavor." Sit quietly for a few moments and try to sense these emotions in your heart and body. Which is dominant for you? What do these sensations tell you about your internal belief system? What "truth" about yourself are you avoiding looking at? Don't go in with a search light. Go in with a candle and see what beliefs are willing to introduce themselves to you from the shadows.

As memories, fears and stories return to you, make friends with them. Get their names, and if possible figure out the years they were "born." When you think you know what you have been telling yourself, take the time to write it down, and then get ready to have a conversation.

In **The Secret of Emotions**, I said that you couldn't *get rid* of old habits and patterns, you had to *replace* them, instead. Well, the same principle applies to old beliefs.

These beliefs, no matter how absurd, childish or painful, are not your enemy. They developed over time for a reason. They helped you make sense of your world and your place within it.

Once you recognize them, you need to honor them, thank them, and only then gently explain to them why they no longer apply to your life today. You want to take that old belief by the hand, and walk it towards a more mature and functional perspective, not shame it out of existence.

For example, I felt responsible for my parent's divorce. It would be easy to tell myself, "Don't be stupid. It isn't your fault, so just get over it." But then my sense of responsibility would just go into hiding.

Instead, I can tell myself that every child of a divorce feels responsible; that children see themselves as the center of the universe and interpret parental behavior accordingly.

I can remind myself that children need to feel that the universe makes sense and that things don't happen without a cause. It was safer to believe that I was the cause than to believe in a chaotic world.

I can find all of the reasons why I was sure that I was to blame, and then—only then—go back and assure myself that I can know better now. As an adult I can understand adult motivations, I can see the bigger picture, I can put my childhood fears in perspective. "Thank you for helping me make sense of the world, but look at how much more sense the world can make if we look at it this way."

If you are having a difficult time finding replacement beliefs for these old sources of guilt, a professional therapist can help you find alternative perspectives with which to comfort and educate your inner child.

Recognizing and then letting go of the guilt will likely be accompanied by copious amounts of tears. Many of us have been holding in a lot of guilt for a long time. We were afraid that if we ever actually admitted *what* we felt guilty for, we would be proven guilty and punished accordingly. After all, what *is* the punishment for not being worthy to live? Why would we ever want to risk finding out?

The process of forgiving ourselves follows the pattern of feeling our anger and guilt, *recognizing* the source, *validating* our inner child's right to feel these feelings, but then *identifying* the specific injustices that we blamed ourselves for and *changing our beliefs* about them so that we no longer feel the need to punish ourselves. The choice we made was to validate the emotion but redefine the injustice. Our action was to educate ourselves and let go of our need for punishment.

So what do we do when we *can't* redefine our sins or change our beliefs about them? How do we forgive ourselves when we really have done bad things?

The first step is to look at your behavior in the context of the pain, anger, hurt and guilt that informed all of your decisions from early childhood on. When you make choices as to how to act, you are doing it based on who you believe you are. If you are given faulty information about who you are, then that will influence your choices. Forgiveness of anyone, including ourselves, requires a bit of compassion and understanding. But perhaps, before you forgive yourself completely, you do need to consider additional appropriate responses. Your response to your own acts of injustice may need to be similar to your response to other's acts of injustice. We will explore those in a few pages.

But there is a well-established system in place that is designed to help people forgive themselves for their defects of character and the harm that they have caused. It is called *Making Amends*.

If you know anything about twelve-step programs, you probably know that they encourage people to *"make direct amends to all people we have harmed wherever possible, except when to do so would injure them or others."* What you may not know is that it takes the first nine of the twelve steps to prepare for this process.

You may be under the impression that making amends to people is designed to make people feel ashamed and guilty. Actually, the result is just the opposite. It releases shame and guilt, and breaks the emotional bonds that keep us tied to our mistakes.

When we prepare to make amends, we are asked to acknowledge the pain we have caused others. This process invites us to feel compassion for them; to put ourselves in their shoes and imagine what our actions might have felt like from their perspective. This is a powerful exercise that gives us the opportunity to see ourselves through their eyes.

Their view of us mirrors our perception of those who

hurt us. That is, we can imagine them feeling about us the same way as we feel about those who hurt us.

Seeing ourselves as both the abuser and the abused breaks down barriers. We begin to realize that abusers are often just victims who are doing the only thing they know how to do. Understanding that abuse is a cycle does not excuse our behavior or theirs, but it does make it easier to forgive. The question of blame and the need to hate lose their power over us.

This is a profound and complex process. I don't expect or even advise that you set out to make amends to those you have harmed until you have done a lot of preparatory work. I just wanted you to know that the step is out there, and it does help.

The last bit of advice I have for healing guilt is to encourage you to use affirmations. Once we have introduced ourselves to our deepest, darkest sources of guilt, made friends with them and offered them a new perspective, we can solidify this new perspective in our subconscious by developing phrases that reinforce our new beliefs about ourselves and saying them several times a day. While giving yourself a daily pep-talk may sound silly, it is much less silly than continuing to listen to all of the negative self-talk that is currently bouncing around inside your head. I will talk about affirmations in book three, or you can go online to find more information, or ask your therapist about how to use affirmations to shift your internal beliefs.

Forgiving Others

Exploring the core issues that made us angry and feel guilty about who we are has probably given you a clearer feel for the source of your anger towards other people.

When we look inside to figure out what we feel guilty for, we can see that much of what has worried us for years is truly absurd. We are not evil, worthless, or guilty of any major transgressions against humanity.

When we realize that we are not really evil, we start to wonder how we came to believe these bad things about ourselves in the first place. Some of these absurd beliefs are the result of childish thought processes, but some of them were taught to us by the people we grew up with. In many cases, we were *encouraged*, either directly or indirectly, to believe that there was something wrong with us.

If we think about this for very long, it just might make us angry. After all, who *told* us that we were sinful creatures who deserved to go to hell for eternal punishment? Who made us feel as though *nothing* we did was good enough? Who failed to rescue us from the bullies and abusers that made us feel dirty or ugly or helpless, or guilty?

You see, while a part of us believed that we had a reason to feel guilty and needed to be forgiven, another part of us— sometimes stronger, sometimes beaten down—knew that we were innocent. *That* part of us is angry. *That* part recognizes the fact that we were treated unjustly and accused of wrongs we did not commit or could not control. *That* part knows that we were lied to about our nobility and our humanity and our essential goodness.

That part needs to learn how to forgive others.

Just as a quick reminder:
Forgiveness is a willingness to acknowledge anger, but let go of resentment.

Resentment is an emotional investment in a specific outcome that is never achieved. Holding onto resentment is the result of feeling anger but not following through to positive action.

Working through our anger towards others follows the same progression we've been talking about. First, you allow yourself to feel the feeling. Second, you recognize the source. As with your anger at yourself, the source of your anger may include very old injustices that are difficult to name, as well as current or ongoing injustices in your daily life. In either case, you need to validate your right to be angry before you can begin to sort out the details of the specific injustice. Whether your are angry at your mother for not supporting you when you were young, or your spouse for not supporting you today, you need to accept that anger as valid in order to give yourself permission to explore just *how* valid the anger may or may not be.

Once we identify the specific injustice that has sparked our anger, we then choose an appropriate response and take positive action.

Identifying the Specific Injustice

Up until now, I have been defining anger as an emotional response to the absence of justice. While it is important for us to validate a feeling of anger as a legitimate response to a real injustice so that we can overcome the mental fog of resistance, fear and anger, once we have validated our feelings, it is time to turn on our rational minds and confess the obvious:

Anger is an emotional response to the *perceived* absence of justice.

In order to continue the process of resolving our anger we need to identify the specific injustice and choose an appropriate response. When we reach the stage of identifying the specific injustice that we want to resolve, we may discover that, with the fog of resistance, fear and anger gone, it really *is* an injustice. We may also come to realize that it is *not*.

So the next step is to assess our perception of the experience that has generated our feelings of anger.

As I've said, anger is a sensation. It is *only* a sensation. It tells you that you have perceived an injustice in your life. Since justice is an important spiritual principle, anger is a very valuable tool for understanding your social environment.

BUT... anger doesn't tell you how big the injustice is. It doesn't tell you how accurate your perception is. It doesn't tell you what the other person's motivations were. It doesn't tell you what you should do about it. All it does is let you know that something doesn't feel fair.

Think of it like the smell of smoke. When you smell smoke, you don't throw your arms in the air and go running in circles screaming, "FIRE!" You use the information to guide you while you investigate your surroundings. The purpose of anger is not to get you all riled up and agitated. It is to give you useful information and the energy you need to act on it. When you feel angry, use this information to guide your rational exploration of your current situation. Why are you angry? What triggered your emotional sensation?

In order to get an accurate picture of the source of a current feeling of anger, you need to be able to distinguish it from two related kinds of anger: Displaced Anger and Rage.

Displaced anger is when we are angry at one person or situation, but we project that anger onto someone or something else. There is a classic cartoon in four panels: In the first, a boss yells at a man. In the second, the man yells at his wife. The wife yells at her child, and the child kicks the dog. When I described this cartoon to a class of fifth-graders, they immediately understood the message. "So when my dad yells at me, he might not really be angry at me?" one kid asked. It broke my heart to hear the question, but the realization that he understood the idea gave me hope for his future.

We displace our anger most frequently when the cause of the injustice is more powerful than we are. To protest the injustices we receive from parents, teachers, clergy, bosses, bullies, police, or city hall would just invite additional punishment, and so we either express it towards someone even less powerful than we are, or we store it up as depression or rage.

The sensation of *healthy* anger is in proportion to the size of the injustice you are facing at this moment in time. The chemicals that shoot through your brain when you experience anger only last about 90 seconds. If your anger is overwhelming or builds over a long period of time, then it is probably rage.

Rage takes the injustice of the moment and throws it on the pile of every other injustice you have ever experienced, producing a literally raging fire of emotion. It is important to deal with the many injustices of your life, but it is impossible to deal with all of them at the same time. If you want to deal with one specific injustice, you will have to set the intense energy of rage aside to be dealt with later. Just knowing that it is *possible* to separate anger from rage can be a source of serenity and strength. It means that you can acknowledge the injustices of your past without wrestling with them every time something goes wrong. By dealing with one source of anger at a time, even deep and debilitating rage can be resolved and healed.

When you have identified a single issue or source of injustice that you want to resolve—and you are sure it isn't the victim of displaced anger—then you are ready to take the next two steps: choosing a response, and taking positive action. Choosing an appropriate response is dependent on the answers to the following questions:

1) Are my perceptions accurate—would it still seem unjust from a different perspective?
2) Is there anything reasonable and non-inflammatory I can do to correct the injustice?
3) Can I let go of my need to respond to this injustice?
4) Can I find a way to look past the injustice and love the person behind it?
5) Can I see something positive that came out of it?

Mentally Assessing
Your Emotional Perceptions

Anger is the result of a *perceived* injustice. Sometimes what we perceive is inaccurate. Sometimes what we perceive is colored by our beliefs, by immaturity, by lack of information, or lack of experience. There are many situations, for example, that would seem unfair to a child that, to an adult, would seem perfectly reasonable. As a child, you had a right to be angry, but when you remember this source of anger as an adult, you can understand it and therefore let go of the emotional charge.

There are also situations that adults experience that seem completely unfair from one perspective, but are understandable when seen from a different perspective or when more information is available. For example, if you think someone has hung up the phone on you, this belief will color your perception. What a mean thing to do! If you later find out that their cell phone battery died, then anger can evaporate in an instant.

It is not what *happens* to us that makes us angry, it is our perception that someone has treated us unjustly. As we mature, we become better at distinguishing between intentional harm and accidents; between malicious intent and distracted thoughtlessness.

Acquiring the virtues of patience, compassion, flexibility and objectivity can assist in this process and help to mitigate or eliminate anger through understanding. We may decide that what our parents did to us really wasn't so bad. That doesn't change the pain we felt at the time, but it does help us let go of the anger now. We may realize that our expectations in life were naturally immature as children, and may currently be unreasonable as adults. We don't always get what we want, but that doesn't mean life is unfair.

Many of us live our lives feeling defensive for good reason. We have not been treated well. But this attitude can be counter-productive. If we already feel victimized or unworthy, then we live in a constant state of needing positive feedback from others. *Anything* less than that can feel like an attack, and it can keep us feeling resentful and angry. In this condition, even "have a nice day" can be perceived as an unjust imposition, and really tick us off.

When *we know* that we are good, noble souls, it becomes easier to forgive the thousands of little slights we can encounter or perceive in a confused and distracted world. We don't take things so personally. It becomes easier to forgive.

Separating the injustice from the blame

I have said that anger is a natural response to injustice, but what *is* injustice, really?

Each of us is a noble child of God. We all deserve to receive kindness, respect and encouragement. We deserve safety, security, education, food and shelter. We feel sad when the virtues of God are absent from our lives. We feel angry when those virtues are denied to us through the actions of another person.

In other words, we are *sad* when we feel that there is an absence of virtues in our lives, but we feel *angry* when we convince ourselves that it is someone else's fault. So anger is a two-step process: first the recognition that we aren't receiving the virtues that we deserve, and second, the blaming of someone else.

As children, we are relatively powerless, so if there is a lack of kindness, encouragement, security or food, it probably *is* someone else's fault. The ability to recognize that you deserve these things is very important for your spiritual growth. The need to blame is *not* so important. When we understand that what we are feeling is the absence of the virtues we needed, we can begin to consider the fact that no one can give us something that they, themselves, do not already have. How does one blame one's parents for not passing on a set of qualities that they never received from their parents?

We are absolutely right to be angry. But what is the point of holding on to resentment? What positive outcome can we possibly imagine might be the result?

As adults, we have a great deal of control over the virtues in our lives. Anger tells us that someone may be trying to threaten our security, self-esteem, or other virtues, but in most situations, *we* are the ones who control whether or not they succeed. Someone may insult us, but *we* choose whether to let it affect our self-esteem. Someone may cut us off in traffic, but unless they actually cause an accident, it is *we* who decide whether to be distracted the rest of the drive home. Someone may leave the toilet seat up, but *we* can interpret that as a sign of forgetfulness, or a sign of disrespect. The ability to recognize rudeness, recklessness and forgetfulness is a valuable skill which anger helps us develop. The desire to blame, retaliate or fume over these lapses is not so helpful.

Turning Judgment into Discernment

In **The Secret of Emotions**, I explained how perfection-ism and black-and-white thinking kept us in a constant state of failure, and therefore kept us ashamed. A similar dynamic happens in our relationship with others. We are taught to judge people and actions as either good or bad, and then allow ourselves to get angry or offended based on that judgment.

Our tendency to get angry is affected by three dynamics. First is our sensitivity to unjust behavior, second is the starkness of our division between acceptable and unacceptable behavior, and third is our tendency to globalize.

People who have been hurt a lot as children tend to swing in one of two opposite directions. Either they numb themselves to the pain of injustice and become doormats, or they become hyper-sensitive to injustice and become prickly complainers or rage-aholics. Neither extreme is helpful.

The ability to recognize rudeness goes hand-in-hand with the ability to recognize kindness. Being able to discern *exactly* how kind a person is on a scale from one to a hundred would be very useful. It would help you choose who to spend your time with, and even more important, it would help you identify what behaviors you should practice.

Here is where we get into trouble: if, on that scale from one to a hundred, we say, "I prefer to be around people between ninety-five and one hundred," then we are being way too sensitive to imperfections and will constantly be disappointed by the normal humans who populate our lives.

Or, if we say, "Anyone who falls below fifty is rude and deserves to be punished," then we are being judgmental, and will carry resentments towards all sorts of people.

We are also globalizing based on one virtue. We could, for example, say instead, "That person has horrible manners, but he tells funny jokes and is a great dancer."

When we do all three—have high expectations, have strong judgments against anyone who falls below them, and judge a person's entire character based on one failure to practice a particular virtue, then we doom ourselves to being constantly angry at everyone. We have also placed our own serenity firmly in the hands of every stranger we meet.

The way we perceive injustice affects our ability to forgive in the same way that the way we perceive right and wrong affects our ability to heal shame.

To counteract this common tendency, some forgiveness counselors recommend instantly forgiving everyone all the time for everything. They say that, since every experience is a learning experience, all injustice is an illusion.

I disagree.

The only way to learn from an experience is to identify it accurately and then respond appropriately. Anger tells us that we are not receiving something that we deserve. If we ignore the anger, we will never know what it is we've lost. Instead I recommend using discernment. Discernment allows us to identify what is missing, protect what is threatened, strengthen all needed virtues, and only *then* let go of any need to pursue additional outcomes. In other words, discernment allows us to both change our perception and *change the situation.*

Looking at the experiences that have hurt us from another perspective, separating injustice from blame and using discernment rather than judgment are all ways of reassessing our perceptions. In many cases, the injustice will now seem so small that it no longer calls for a response. Our positive action will be to let go of any need for vindication, restitution, revenge or apology. The messenger was wrong; it was a misunderstanding; or it wasn't worth worrying about. Anger has been dismissed—with gratitude—but dismissed all the same.

But sometimes the messenger is right.

Choosing a Response

Not all injustices are the result of misunderstandings or minor irritations. Sometimes situations really are significantly and painfully unjust. There is a lot of injustice in the world, so chances are good that you've experienced your share. What do you do then?

You've probably heard of the Serenity Prayer:

"God grant me the serenity to accept the things I cannot change, the courage to change the things I can and the wisdom to know the difference."

Once we have determined that the specific injustice that caused our anger is real and significant, then it is time to choose an *appropriate* response. Is there something you can do that would actually make the situation better for everyone? Often the answer is *No*, in which case, you need to take a deep breath and move on to letting go and finding a way to forgive the person involved. But sometimes the answer is *Yes*.

Often these are times when the injustice is ongoing. Taking action can protect us or someone else from physical, emotional or spiritual harm.

Children don't have the resources to correct most unjust situations, but as adults we have an obligation to at least consider trying. Even if we can't fix an entire problem, we can make an effort. Helping even a little bit can give us a sense of power and accomplishment that tempers our anger. Shame and depression are often linked to feelings of powerlessness. It is amazing how even little efforts in the cause of justice can lift our spirits and discharge our anger.

We must be careful, though, that our efforts at correcting an injustice are not excuses for exacting revenge instead.

Revenge is not about correcting a situation, it is about punishing a person by causing them harm. The desire for revenge is unhealthy for several reasons.

First, revenge does not resolve anger, it simply perpetuates the cycle of abuse. Healing an injustice is not about punishing the perpetrator, but simply protecting the victim, whether it is yourself or another. If the injustice is severe enough, then it is the job of the courts to punish.

Second, the desire for revenge actually increases our feelings of powerlessness. Protecting ourselves is something we have a fair amount of control over, so in taking steps toward this, we can satisfy our need to respond and let go of resentment. However, if our goal is punishment, we are emotionally invested in a type of response that we have little legitimate control over. While we wait for the slow wheels of justice to turn, our resentment will fester and grow, making us more angry, feeling less in control of our lives.

Third, it is impossible to feel both compassion and revenge at the same time. Looking forward to someone else's suffering—even if they absolutely deserve it—is a form of spiritual poison.

Putting Your Energy to Better Use

Perhaps you aren't quite ready to let go of your resentments. After all, anger is what gives many people the energy to get up in the morning. But resentment is an emotional investment in an outcome. What if you took all of that investment, all of that emotional energy, and directed it towards a *different* outcome—one that was still directly related to the injustice you suffered, but was not about revenge, punishment, or even reconciliation?

If we find that there is nothing we can do for the specific situation that we faced or are facing, perhaps there are things we can do in a related area that can make us feel that we are helping to address a larger injustice than our own. Volunteering at shelters, doing educational work with children, becoming a mentor in a youth program or sponsor in a twelve-step program can all be manifestations of the "courage to change the things I can."

The outcome we dedicate ourselves to can also be more personal. Injustice robs us of the opportunity to experience important virtues. An appropriate response would be to learn everything you can about the virtues that were denied you in the past, and commit yourself to developing them to the fullest in the years ahead. Every challenge we face in life is an opportunity to learn and grow. Anger is like a flashing red arrow pointing to the challenges in your life that you are being invited to learn from. Not everyone is blessed with such clear road signs on the path of spiritual growth. Use them.

Perhaps more clearly than anything else, anger tells us that our lives have been devoid of compassion. The best response to injustice is an effort to develop compassion—if not compassion for the people who hurt you, then perhaps for the many like them that you meet at twelve-step meetings, in your daily life, or when looking in the mirror. You are not the same as the people who hurt you, and for that you can be grateful. But you carry a part of them around with you. Developing compassion for others will help you feel it for yourself.

I will be discussing compassion in great detail in the next section, but I wanted to mention it a couple of times in this section on forgiveness, because it takes on a different character when combined with forgiveness. Feeling compassion for those who have hurt us is like putting a blowtorch to a candle. It melts the resistance and rearranges everything.

⚘

When the Appropriate Response Is No Response

Many situations are so far in the past or are so large that we have no appropriate way to respond to them. What do we do then?

When the injustice is real and there is nothing you can do about it, then you *could* stew in your anger forever and let it eat away at your faith and joy. But that wouldn't be very helpful. Instead, you could turn your need to respond over to God.

That doesn't mean that you pray to God that the guilty party be hit with a lightning bolt or sent to hell. It means that you allow your faith in a higher justice—in the Karmic Principle of *you reap what you sow*—to melt the chains of resentment that keep you attached to the one who wronged you.

The recovery community of twelve-step programs encourages people to, "Let go and let God." That one phrase has helped keep millions of people sane and sober. It is the *surest* way to let go of resentments and allow the peace and serenity of forgiveness to seep into our souls. Yet, for many people, it is also the hardest.

At first, the act of letting go might just be a grudging, "OK, I'll stop obsessing about this and let God handle it. God will make sure they reap what they sow."

But the deeper meaning of *you reap what you sow* is that if you sow true forgiveness and compassion and positive thoughts towards those who have hurt you, that is what your life will be filled with. That is why the highest form of forgiveness is more than simply letting go of resentment, it is a stepping past the injustice and looking for the lost child of God who perpetrated it.

This is where experience in a twelve-step community can once again be helpful. It can give you the experience of loving and forgiving people who have made terrible mistakes in their lives, including ones that may have hurt others. It is easier to forgive strangers because what makes forgiveness difficult is not the size of the injustice, but the size of our emotional investment in responding to it. When we don't have personal resentments to get in the way, we can see the good person behind the unjust act or the hurtful mistake. That experience makes it easier for us to see the good in the people who have hurt us and been unjust.

One of the side benefits of developing this capacity for forgiveness is that we can then apply it to our other tools for resolving anger. An attitude of compassionate forgiveness provides us with a new perspective on our old hurts. It is easier to see things from another person's point of view if we have already forgiven them and are giving them the benefit of the doubt.

Likewise, compassionate forgiveness makes it easier to rectify unjust situations because we approach them in a more loving, non-confrontational manner. We look for win-win solutions to problems rather than exacting revenge on those who may have hurt us in the past.

❧

Permission to Forgive

Why is it that many people resist this most basic kind of forgiveness? What are we afraid might happen if we just "let it go?"

I think our deepest fear is that if we forgive someone, what we are really doing is ignoring the injustice, and that by doing that we are saying that the injustice was not real, it did not matter, or that it was not really an injustice at all.

Our fear is that to forgive is to accept that we deserved what happened to us.

We began the process of dealing with our anger by validating the legitimacy of our feelings. Now that we have looked at our experiences from different perspectives and explored different possible responses—including understanding and compassion—we can remove our final barriers to forgiveness by validating our *understanding* of our experience at the end of the process. This validation encompasses our feelings, our interpretation of the injustice, the response we have chosen and the actions we are taking.

Once again I encourage you to talk to a therapist or share with a twelve-step group, or at least have a gripe session with a close friend *before* your final effort to let go of anger and resentment. You need to hear someone say—in words or with their silent encouragement, *"I'm so sorry that happened to you. You did not deserve to be treated that way."*

This *external validation* can go a long way in helping you get rid of anger and resentment.

This is where I believe a good therapist is better suited to help than friends or recovery groups because a therapist can both be objective, and say *the words you need to hear.*

A therapist can help you through the steps of process-ing anger. They can help you determine if what you experi-enced was an injustice or if you need to change your per-spective. They can help you find a safe and reasonable course of action to take. They can listen to you describe the injus-tice and help you can name it so that you can let it go.

Friends are not objective, and may try to take sides or give advice on how to get revenge. In twelve-step groups, as I've said, people don't generally speak directly to one an-other after sharing—though you can often see compassion and empathy in their eyes.

Serious injustices, though—especially ones that you dig up from your past—really require an objective witness who can verbalize the legitimacy of your pain. That's why a good therapist can remove one of the biggest obstacles to forgive-ness. You can let go of the anger because it has been made real. It exists outside of your inner world because someone else has perceived the injustice and named it as such.

In fact, a therapist can often give the injustice an actual name. You might be surprised how healing this can be. Yes, that is *emotional abuse*. Yes, that is *spiritual abuse*. Yes, that is *sexual abuse*. Yes, that was *controlling* and *manipulative*. Yes, that was *abandonment*. Yes, the threat of violence is still *vio-lence*. Yes, you were right to be frightened and angry for be-ing treated that way. Yes, you can forgive this, even though it was an injustice. That is what forgiveness means.

Can it really be this easy? Sometimes, yes.

Resentment is an emotional investment in an outcome. Sometimes, sincere validation is the only outcome that you really need. Wrestling with your fears and anger, betraying family secrets, asking for help, these are the hard parts. Once your pain is validated, forgiveness and letting go often come easily. Validation gives you permission to forgive.

This kind of letting go is exactly the opposite of the kind of letting go you did when you changed your perceptions. In the *first* case, you looked at what happened to you and realized that what you had perceived as an injustice when you were a child was not unjust after all. In *this* case, however, you look at what happened and receive external confirmation that it really *was* unjust. It is the *validation* of your perceptions that allows you to say *"I was right. They were wrong. Now I can give myself permission to stop clinging to the proof that I was wronged and move on."*

How do we know when we have succeeded in forgiving?

As I said when describing people's misunderstandings about forgiveness, forgiving does not mean that you like, trust, or want to spend time with the person who hurt you. It doesn't mean that you have forgotten what has happened or will make yourself vulnerable to future injustices. All it means is that you are no longer emotionally invested in the injustice. Thinking about the person or the event does not give you a twinge of anxiety, a rush of adrenaline, or an elevated heart rate. You no longer dwell on the event, or relive it in your mind. You do not feel the need to respond to the person or event in word or deed, nor do you feel the need to *avoid* thinking about them. Your emotional serenity no longer has anything to do with that particular situation.

It is a great feeling.

The first book in this series, **The Secret of Emotions**, focused on the relationship between emotions and virtues, and looked particularly at the role of shame in pushing us toward unhealthy behaviors. This book has expanded the focus from just shame to shame and three other emotions that tell us that there is something wrong: anger, loneliness and fear. The first two sections have looked at the benefits of honesty in healing shame and forgiveness in healing anger and shame. Let's move on, now, to exploring the role of compassion in healing anger, shame and loneliness. I've already mentioned how compassion and forgiveness can work together to help us understand ourselves and those who have hurt us. Now let's look more deeply at what compassion is and how it can serve us.

Compassion

Compassion is sometimes the fatal capacity for feeling what it is like to live inside somebody else's skin. It is the knowledge that there can never really be any peace and joy for me until there is peace and joy finally for you too.   — *Frederick Buechner*

My dictionary defines compassion as a "sympathetic concern for another person's pain or suffering." It defines "sympathetic" as the ability to feel what another person is feeling. So compassion is concern for another person's pain and suffering that is motivated not only by an *intellectual* appreciation of his difficulty, but by a shared *emotional* response to it. This is a much more profound and meaningful definition than many are comfortable with. Some would prefer to place compassion alongside pity, concern or kindness, as an activity that can be done at arm's length. But the mingling of emotions is what distinguishes compassion from these other virtues, and is also what makes it such a fascinating subject of exploration.

By defining compassion in terms that include shared emotions, we change the dynamics of our response. We behave differently when we feel another person's pain than if we simply pity him or her.

There is another reason for making a distinction between compassion and pity, concern or kindness. The word itself can be broken down into the prefix *"com,"* meaning "with or together"—as in *com*munication, *com*munity, and com*mune* (as in prayer)—and *"passion,"* which means strong feelings or emotions. So *compassion* literally means to have a strong emotion together with another person. Pity, on the other hand, means to feel sorry for someone. We can feel *pity* for someone who is blissfully unaware that he or she is the recipient of our sorrowful attention. Pity can be self-righteous and even cruel. Compassion can't be. Compassion requires an act of transcendence—a temporary and perhaps even miniscule setting aside of oneself in order to perceive life for a moment through another person's heart.

The Five Steps of Compassion

There are five steps in the process of practicing compassion. For some they may take a lifetime to learn, while for others they can be traveled in the twinkling of an eye.

First, you see another person from your own perspective. We all start here.

Second, you recognize some point of unity or commonality between you. This will be easier with some people than others, but we all share our common humanity.

Third, you use this point of commonality to shift your perspective and begin to see them and their situation from *their* perspective.

Fourth, when you begin to *see* the world from their perspective, you will begin to *feel* the world from their perspective because our feelings are shaped by the virtues we perceive in our environment.

Fifth, your feelings will motivate you to act. Perhaps all you will be able to do is express sincere concern, but it is also possible that you have knowledge or resources that the person whose feelings you share does not have. Being able to perceive a situation from *two* perspectives creates an increased capacity for wisdom and understanding.

Why Practice Compassion?

If you want others to be happy, practice compassion. If you want to be happy, practice compassion.   — The Dalai Lama

When we think of practicing compassion, we tend to think of it as an obligation. We are compassionate for the sake of someone else. But that is only half the equation.

One of the themes of this book is that the practice of virtues serves us in two ways. First, virtues heal our emotional pain by filling our lives with the qualities that have been missing. So honesty helps heal the shame that came from carrying secrets and forgiveness heals the pain of anger and resentment. Likewise, compassion is a wonderful tool for helping us feel connected and easing our loneliness.

But virtues also serve another function: they offer us positive activities and enjoyable sensations to replace the activities and sensations that generated and reinforced our shame. In this regard, honesty and forgiveness make us feel good, but compassion? Compassion makes us feel amazing.

Compassion helps us tear down the walls of isolation that keep us separated from the people around us and make us feel lonely. The first thing we notice is that we no longer feel lonely, but feeling connected is *more* than just not feeling bad.

Compassion allows us to experience the sensation of *transcendence*—that is, the feeling of being connected to something *bigger* than ourselves. This is not a metaphysical connection, but a heart connection that expands our perspective of our place in the universe. This, according to happiness research, is one of the keys to deep life satisfaction.

By connecting to people and experiences that are bigger than we are, we also gain access to a source of wisdom that can guide our choices and protect us from foolish mistakes.

Combined, these gifts of compassion go beyond healing old hurts. They bring us true joy.

The Science of Compassion

"By compassion we make others' misery our own, and so, by relieving them, we relieve ourselves also." — Thomas Browne, Sr.

One of ways in which shame keeps a grip on us is through our sense of isolation. When we believe that no one else has done what we have done or felt what we have felt, then we feel even more broken and ashamed. This shame, in turn, acts as a wall around us to keep us from even *trying* to connect with others. Shame and isolation work together to build a wall of loneliness between us and everyone else. Compassion breaks down that wall.

Practicing honesty by sharing your story and listening to others' stories allows you to *see* that you are not alone; that other people have had experiences similar to yours, but practicing compassion allows you to *feel* that you are not alone by recognizing that even when experiences are different, the feelings are the same.

How can we do that? How can we possibly *know* what someone else is feeling if we have not had the exact same experience? How can we *feel* what they are feeling if we are not them? If I have not lost my friend, or my job or my health or my home, how is it that I can *feel* your loss?

We know how to *think* what another person is thinking. We simply ask them to explain their thoughts, and in the process of listening, we end up thinking the same thing (though we may think that they are wrong, we are, nevertheless, thinking the same thoughts.) But how do we get our hearts to respond with the same feeling that another person is feeling? Even if they tell us what they think their emotion is, "knowing" and "feeling" are not the same thing.

I would like to offer three different theories as to how emotions can be shared, based on different understandings of how humans are connected to one another. The first is for people who believe we are connected in an abstract, conceptual way; the second is for people who feel we are emotionally connected; and the third is for the more metaphysically minded who believe we are all spiritually united.

The theories on how one person's emotional state can create a parallel response in another person's heart include:

1. The use of cues
   a. Physical cues
   b. Psychological cues
   c. Spiritual cues
2. Emotional resonance
3. Psychic connection

Physical Cues and Mirror Neurons.

On one level, we can explain our capacity for compassion in terms of neurology. It would appear that we are biologically hard-wired for compassion. That's right. It is in our DNA to identify with the feelings of others. This may not be obvious from your personal experience, but it *is* the lesson of recent scientific studies. These studies aren't from the schools of psychology or sociology. They are studies of the way our brains respond to the actions of the people around us.

The lessons of these studies are both astonishing, and so obvious that we all understand them intuitively.

If someone near us stubs their toe, we wince.

If they smile at us, we instinctively smile back.

If they laugh enthusiastically, we start to laugh.

If they cry, we fight back tears.

If we watch them do a running long-jump, our muscles tense as they run and relax when we see them land.

From gross physical movement to subtle emotional cues, humans are hard-wired to mirror the actions of the people around them. Neurologists theorize that, not just humans, but other animals as well, have "mirror neurons" that fire in the brain in areas that correspond to the actions that we observe.

In humans, this mirroring process is not just about physical actions, but responds to perceived intentions as well. For example, the brain reacts differently if it sees a person pick up a cup, pick up a cup in order to take a drink, or pick up a cup in order to clear a table of dirty dishes. The parts of the brain that react correspond to the parts of the brain that would activate if the observer were to do the behavior him or herself—*for the same reason.*

What this means is that when you watch another person's actions, *you identify with him or her whether you want to or not.* If a person is hurt, your body *will* respond. If a person is feeling strong emotions, your body *will* mirror those emotions to some degree.

We all know this. We've known it for centuries. But until now it has been an intuitive knowledge that we could dismiss and ignore. Now we have hard scientific proof that we are all strongly influenced by the actions and emotions of the people around us.*

In fact, we are not just *influenced.* It is as though a shadow part of ourselves steps into the other person and goes through the same motions and *emotions* as they do. In doing so, do we learn, experience, perceive or feel what they do? If watching a golfer swing his club makes neurons fire in our brains,

---

* *Do a web search for Mirror Neurons for a host of articles on this rapidly growing field of research.*

does that make us a better golfer too? Scientists seem to think it might. And if watching a mother care for her child makes our neurons fire in ways that are different from watching her bake a cake, then how does that change us?

The grand implications are somewhat staggering. Knowing about this innate capacity for connecting with others gives us a powerful tool for developing our compassion— especially when we understand that this capacity to identify with others is not limited to those we see in person, or even those we see in videos, but also those we experience in our imaginations.

If we want to develop our capacity for compassion, then one way is to surround ourselves with compassionate people to emulate, but another way is to choose uplifting sources of entertainment. There are many wonderful movies, documentaries and books that provide opportunities for us to reflect upon positive behavior, be moved by expression of virtue, and feel compassion for people who can expand our sense of connection with the world. The trick is to make the effort to surround ourselves with *positive* images, *positive* emotions, and *positive* people. Then when our mirror neurons kick in and we are drawn into a compassionate connection with the world around us, it will be a rewarding and enlightening experience.

The alternative is to allow the world to subject us its barrage of negative images, stories and people.

When we understand the power of watching, we grasp the importance of making conscious choices about what we put in front of our eyes. When we understand our innate tendency to step into the shoes of the people we spend time with, we grasp the importance of choosing our friends and activities wisely.

This book is not the place to explore all of the ways in which we are influenced by the TV shows, movies and videos we watch, or the books we read and the games we play, but we would be foolish to try to improve our behavior and spiritualize our lives without considering the power of that influence.

I think that the prevalence of sex and violence and simple *meanness* in the visual images we are bombarded with every day has two contradictory effects on us.

First of all, we are forced to desensitize ourselves against the violence and cruelty we see everywhere—both in the name of humor and in the name of excitement. If we are hard-wired to wince when we see someone stub their toe or hit their head, then how can we possibly sit through *The Three Stooges, Tom and Jerry, America's Funniest Home Videos, Home Alone,* or any of the thousands of other videos that use violence as a form of humor, without working mightily to resist our urge to feel compassion?

The fact is, none of these forms of entertainment are funny. They are incredibly stressful, and one of the tools our bodies use to release stress is to exhale explosively in something resembling laughter. Okay, it *is* laughter, but there is happy laughter and *laugh so you don't cry* laughter.*

When we surround ourselves with slapstick humor, it trains us to distance ourselves from other people's pain. This is just as true in the case of emotional violence. Most situation comedies rely on a constant stream of insults and put-downs. Our natural response to this kind of personal attack is an emotional wince. Then we feel the relief of realizing that the insult was not directed at us, but at some poor schmuck on the screen, and we release the tension with a laugh. We are grateful that we *don't* identify with him or her (too much, anyway), and remind ourselves to *not* feel too

---

Positive laughter also releases stress, but it is the positive stress of encountering the delight of the unexpected. The secret of humor is surprise.

much compassion. That the poor schmuck doesn't dissolve in a puddle of tears tells us that insults aren't that bad after all, as long as you don't care about the person being insulted (and it isn't you).

Likewise, violent images in adventure, mystery and horror movies use our natural "wince response" to get our bodies all worked up, and then convince us that we are excited and having fun.

We aren't excited. We are expending energy to try to *not* identify with all of the pain we are seeing so that we are not overwhelmed. We are actively working to *not* allow our natural compassion to send us running from the theater.

All that this does is make it easier to ignore *real* pain and suffering when we see them on the news, or on the street in front of us. And we call it entertainment because, as I said earlier, *any* sensation is better than no sensation at all.

We are so afraid of *real* compassion, and so ignorant of how to generate positive *spiritual* sensations that we allow ourselves to be manipulated to accept these base and ugly sensations as the best entertainment we have.

So, on one hand, video images desensitize us to feeling other people's pain. On the *other* hand, they manipulate us to try to *make* us feel other people's sexual impulses. If watching a person put a cup of water up to his lips causes our mirror neurons to fire in a way that resembles *our* taking a drink, *what* in heaven's name happens in our brains when we watch two people kiss on a 40-foot screen—or four people have meaningless intercourse on a computer screen?

If, as studies have shown, our brains react not just to the movement of limbs, but to the perceived *intention* behind those movements, then watching a well-acted drama in which two people express their sincere love and commitment to one another with a kiss might actually be *good* for our ability to identify with healthy relationships.

On the other hand, watching people have meaningless sex for the purpose of getting paid to make a video might leave one feeling both aroused and empty. What effect would *this* have on one's ability to feel compassion? How do these base and ugly sensations compare to the feelings our hearts truly long for? We deserve better.

The Art of Compassion

Mirror neurons cause us to identify with the physical actions of others whether we want to or not, whether we choose to or not, whether we are conscious of it or not. But true compassion is literally not a knee-jerk reaction. It is a choice to create a bond with another person. We can choose to numb, distract or ignore our biological reaction to another person's experience, or we can embrace it. Most people prefer to avoid pain and sadness, so a willing desire to experience the same emotion as someone who is grieving or suffering is an act of great courage and generosity. It requires more than the science of neurons, it requires the art of watching, listening, feeling and *connecting*.

Physical Cues

Having chosen to express compassion, I can choose to augment my mirror neurons' natural response by looking for a wide range of cues to tell me what you are feeling. The most obvious cue is your physical state. Tears, crying, sobbing, trembling, flushed skin, weakness, are all clear signs of an emotional crisis. These are the cues that our mirror neurons are most likely to reflect. But stress, depression, pain, anxiety, hopelessness, and fear *also* have clear physical signs for those who are attentive enough to notice them. People who grew up in dysfunctional or abusive families may have particularly well-developed "emotional radar" because their very survival was dependent upon accurately reading the non-verbal signals that forecast their parents' emotional state. The twitch of a lip, the speed of a movement, or the texture of a voice can all provide innumerable clues as to what a person is feeling.

There may even be much more subtle physical cues to help people in close proximity to loved ones pick up on the emotional state of those they care for. They say that animals can smell fear and it is true. Humans release unique scents and odorless pheromones in accordance with our emotional states. Though we may be consciously oblivious to these subtle cues, millions of years of biology may provide unexplored subconscious chemical hints as to the emotions of our companions.

Psychological Cues

In addition to purely physical cues, we can use our minds to tease out psychological cues as to what another person is feeling. Most obviously, we can either observe their situation, or ask them point-blank what they are feeling. If someone's dog is missing and they say they are worried sick about it, then you have a pretty good starting place for figuring out what they are feeling. Clarifying questions can help fine-tune the exact emotional state. "How long has it been missing? How long have you owned it? Is it an inside pet or an outside guard dog? Have you ever lost a pet before? Do you have other pets? Have you always had dogs?" etc. Now if you love dogs too, then this information may make it easier to create an emotional connection. If you don't like dogs, then an emotional twenty-questions may create more distance than compassion. Psychologists are experts at drawing people out so that not only does the therapist have a clear understanding of the emotion involved, but the patient himself also has a more precise label for his emotional state.

Spiritual Cues

The final cues that we can use to figure out what another person is feeling are spiritual. Though the word spiritual often implies some kind of metaphysical connection, in this context, spiritual cues can be used even if we assume that there is absolutely no direct spiritual connection between the people involved.

Compassion invites us to see ourselves in another person, and in so doing, see the world through their eyes and feel the world through their heart. In the process, hearts become one. They feel the same feelings because they perceive the same spiritual need, and are pulled by the same longings.

In other words, since feelings are a response to the presence or absence of a *virtue*, it is the *virtue*, not the specific experience, that generates the feeling. That means that we can feel what someone else is feeling even when we have not had the same experience because we have longed for the same virtues that they long for, and rejoice in the same virtues that they rejoice in. When we listen to their stories, a part of us is saying, "Yes, that is the virtue I would recognize; that is the loss I would identify; that is the injustice I would perceive in that situation." And in recognizing, identifying and perceiving the presence or absence of these qualities, our own hearts are moved to generate appropriate sensations. We feel along *with* them, and even when it hurts, it feels good.

Through this compassion, we know that our shared longing for virtues connects us to other people, even though our material circumstances may be very different.

From this understanding of emotions, we can see that in order to feel the same thing as someone else, we don't necessarily even need to know what they are feeling. What we need to know is what virtues are present, and what virtues have been lost to them. Faced with injustice, we, too, will feel angry. Faced with the loss of something good and true, we, too, will feel great sadness and loss.

To illustrate this concept, I must again turn to my experience with a twelve-step program. I was sitting in a meeting for cocaine addicts. I was not a cocaine addict, but when you are in recovery, you take the meeting that is there when you need one. As a non-addict, I was trying to hold myself at arm's-length from "those people" while still participating in the process.

Then a young woman shared. She talked about living on the street, and her family and her shame, and her efforts at recovery, and the things she was learning... and somewhere in the middle of the story, I realized that there was no "arm's-length" between us. There was not a hair's-breadth difference between her pain and mine; between her shame and mine; between her longing for God and mine.

Paradoxically, sharing this woman's pain was one of the most joyful experiences of my life. It broke down barriers and helped me see myself as part of an interconnected web of life. It helped me transcend my limited vision of myself.

Compassion as Emotional Resonance

Okay, now that I have established the fact that compassion is possible even if there is no underlying spiritual connection between human hearts and minds, allow me to take a step into the more esoteric field of emotional resonance.

Resonance is an amazing phenomenon. Here is how it works in the material world. Suppose you have two guitars that are in perfect tune with each other. If you hold them three feet apart and pluck the bottom string on one guitar, the bottom string on the other guitar will start to vibrate. In fact, the top string, which is an octave higher than the bottom string will also start to vibrate—but the ones in between won't. When you see it happen, it seems like magic, but of course it isn't. Sound waves may be invisible, but they are not magic, and their movement of a corresponding string is physics, not psychic. The question is whether the principle of resonance—that objects in tune with each other can influence each other over a distance more easily than objects that are not in tune with each other—can be applied to spiritual realities. If it can, then it provides one more potential means by which one person's emotions can influence another's.

People have talked about "heart strings" and emotional vibrations for thousands of years. In fact, resonance is often referred to as "sympathetic vibrations." I personally believe that our spirits may carry emotional vibrations the way the air carries sound waves, and that people who are emotionally in tune with each other may instinctively vibrate in response to each other's strong emotional states. This is an intermediate level of connection between hearts. It allows for a view of human nature that is essentially independent, but recognizes that there may be a spiritual atmosphere in which we all operate.

Applying the phenomenon of resonance to our emotions allows the possibility of feeling what another person is feeling without being in their physical presence and without understanding the exact nature of their situation. It allows for compassion in silence, and even in ignorance. Certainly this kind of emotional intimacy is rare, but I don't think it is impossible. I do believe that when it operates, it is most often used to fine-tune an emotional understanding gained through more direct contact. Resonance allows us to go from the gross awareness that someone is in pain to the more subtle understanding of exactly how they feel and what they need with a minimum of invasive questions and prying.

Resonance is also a cooperative effort. A person who is in pain is not going to fine-tune his emotions. We are the ones who have to open our hearts to him and adjust our emotional understanding of what he is experiencing until our understanding and his experience harmonize and reinforce one another. A "G" string can't get an out-of-tune "C" string to vibrate, no matter how loud it is played. A man who is suffering cannot move the heart of a selfish person no matter how loud he cries. But if you have ever played an instrument, then you know that special satisfaction that comes from getting your instrument to blend exactly with the one beside you. There is a special purity, a "rightness" that says "Yes! We are on the same wavelength." I think that "magical" sensation is one of the added benefits of experiencing compassion as an act of resonance, not just one of understanding. It is not a requirement, but it is a nice bonus.

Compassion as Spiritual Connection

The third theory of shared emotions is direct psychic connection. Well, perhaps not *conscious* psychic connection, but there is a belief that since we are all connected on a spiritual level, we can gain direct access to another person's strong emotions. Though I don't have much personal experience with this level of connections, I'm not ready to dismiss it as a possibility. After all, when I hit my thumb with a hammer, my whole body jumps—even though my feet had nothing to do with the accident.

According to this view, the reason we can feel compassion for other people is because we are intimately connected to them on a spiritual, psychic level. Their pain is our pain and our pain is their pain. There is certainly plenty of evidence for this view in many spiritual traditions—most obviously in Buddhism, Hinduism and the Bahá'í Faith, but also to a lesser degree in every western religion.

Perhaps all of these views are equally correct. Perhaps people who are apathetic towards one another are like islands, responding only to the strongest mirror neurons, people who respect each other breathe the same spiritual atmosphere and resonate with each other's emotions, and people who love each other deeply are like fingers on one hand or even one soul in many bodies. Perhaps our capacity for compassion increases exponentially with our practice of compassion because it brings us into closer relations and deeper connections with other human hearts.

Whether we are spiritually connected to others, or just emotionally connected, the result is the same: compassion makes us feel part of something bigger than ourselves. It helps us transcend our own limited reality and care deeply about something or someone outside of ourselves. It breaks down the walls of isolation and removes the pain of loneliness.

And through all of that, it makes us wise.

Gaining Wisdom through Compassion

The heaven of divine wisdom is illumined with the two lumi-naries of consultation and compassion.   *— Bahá'u'lláh*

This is a book about emotional healing, but it is also a book about changing our behavior, and gaining a little wisdom can go a long way in avoiding a lot of mistakes.

Wisdom is the virtue that allows us to recognize what virtue is needed in any given situation. Put concisely, wisdom allows us to squeeze maximum spiritual gain out of minimum spiritual pain. It allows us develop our virtues efficiently and effectively. Common wisdom is that wisdom only comes through experience—lots and lots of experience. We need to be able to try many different responses to the same type of tests to see what works and what doesn't. Wisdom, it seems, comes from trial and error.

But does it have to?

We all learn through experience. The more experiences we have, the more mistakes we make. The more mistakes we make, the more we learn and the wiser we become. But life is only so long, and many mistakes are fatal. If I want to learn a lot *and grow old*, then I would be wise to learn as much as I can from *other* people's experiences. Through con-sultation—sharing thoughts, ideas and experiences with people *verbally*—I can experience the world through other people's minds. Through compassion, however, I can expe-rience the world through other people's *hearts*. I can learn how to identify the presence or absence of virtues in differ-ent situations. I can come to feel passion for the virtues that other people love, and grieve the absence of virtues that other people value.

The mind may be able to guess what virtues are present, but it is the heart that is specifically designed to be able to *sense* the presence and absence of virtues. Your mind might be able to guess that a brown liquid in a cup is coffee, but without the sense of taste or smell, it would be difficult to prove. Likewise, there are the virtues that *should* be present in a situation, and then there are the virtues that actually *are.* Our hearts, through our emotional response to a situation, tell us what virtues *we* perceive. But it is only through compassion that we are able to experience the emotional response to the virtues that *someone else* may perceive.

We have all had the experience of expecting a person to react emotionally to a situation in one way, only to discover that they responded completely differently. People's emotional perspective is just as unique, just as personal, and just as *filtered* as their intellectual perspectives. It is *not* that these people are being "illogical." It is that their experience and filters are causing them to sense the presence or absence of a different set of virtues. The only way to understand them— and increase your level of wisdom in the process—is to develop compassion.

Compassion, then, is the virtue that allows us to identify and appreciate a wide range of virtues through our *emotional* connection with other people. When we feel compassion for people who suffer from poverty, sickness, drug addiction, abuse, and other personal loss, then we acquire a great longing for the virtues that would help ease their pain— without ourselves having to suffer from their difficulties. This is a kind of wisdom that no amount of talk will provide.

The capacity for compassion does not only apply to sadness. To feel what another person feels and be compelled to take action can also apply to hope, love and wonder; to courage and conviction; to faith and joy.

When we see a mother cry at the loss of her son, do we not cry? When we see a child laugh in delight and wonder, do we not laugh? Compassion allows us to benefit from *everyone's* experience and be uplifted by *anyone's* joy. It connects us to the entire human race.

"A human being is part of a whole, called by us the Universe, a part limited in time and space. He experiences himself, his thoughts and feelings, as something separated from the rest — a kind of optical delusion of his consciousness.

This delusion is a kind of prison for us, restricting us to our personal desires and to affection for a few persons nearest us. Our task must be to free ourselves from this prison by widening our circles of compassion to embrace all living creatures and the whole of nature in its beauty.

Nobody is able to achieve this completely, but the striving for such achievement is in itself a part of the liberation and a foundation for inner security."   — Albert Einstein

Compassion versus Passion

When we see ourselves in other people, we are focusing on the signs of our common humanity. This encourages us to find the things in other people that make them easy to love, which in turn makes it easier for us to love them. In learning to love the people we see ourselves in, we learn to love ourselves a little more. In loving ourselves and others, we become more loveable. Love attracts love. So compassion helps bring love into our lives.

But there is a twist.

In learning to see ourselves in other people, we are actually doing the *opposite* of what we normally do when we go out searching for passionate love.

In *The Secret of Emotions*, I explained that in spite of our professed interest in finding people that we have common interests with, what most people find themselves attracted to is the *exotic and mysterious stranger*. We shun the boy or girl next door, and dive into relationships with people who make our pulse race.

Focusing on our common humanity, however, *short-circuits* our creation of this fantasy mystery lover. When we see ourselves in others, they are no longer mysterious or frightening. Our common humanity makes them *interesting* rather than exotic. Because of this, the passionate part of compassion does not lead to lust, it leads to understanding and connection and concern and respect.

Feeling what another person feels through compassion puts you both on the same side of a window looking out and emotionally perceiving reality. Because our emotions are designed to respond to the presence of virtues, and virtues are expressions of the attributes of God, at its most pure, compassion allows you to have a shared experience of the Divine. This shared experience has nothing to do with how old or young, cute or ugly, male or female, rich or poor the other person might be. Compassion is not about romance. It is a spiritual connection.

Fear-based romantic feelings, on the other hand, are very different. They are not about a shared experience of reality, but rather sharing the experience of alternating between being predator and prey. *Having* the same feeling is not the same as *sharing* the same feeling. If I'm afraid of you and you are afraid of me, then we are both *having* the same emotion, but we are not standing together looking out at the world. Instead, we are like wolves facing each other and wondering who will be eating whom.

When we see ourselves in others, however, we no longer want to conquer or be conquered. We want to be in harmony. What a pleasant idea!

8

Compassion versus Codependency

So is feeling compassion really a good idea? Won't it just mean that you will get sucked into other people's lives so they can use you to fix their problems? No. That isn't compassion. That is codependency.

Codependency causes us to lose ourselves in another person. Compassion invites us to expand ourselves to include another person. The difference is significant.

In the five steps of compassion I outlined, the third step was to be able to see another person and their situation from *their* perspective. Seeing things from their perspective as well as your own gives you *two* ways of understanding a situation. When we are codependent, we come to see ourselves through another person's eyes, and we are only able to hold onto one perspective—*theirs*.

Codependents define themselves by the way other people see them. To be compassionate, you must first see *yourself* clearly before seeing yourself in others. You are not finding yourself in the way others see you, but rather, you identify with the common virtues that you share with them.

Not everyone who is struggling with emotional healing is codependent, but many are. Fortunately, there are many skills that codependents have developed that can be used in developing compassion—sensitivity to other's needs, listening skills, an interest in helping people in need, etc.

The other good news is that practicing seeing ourselves in others and expressing compassion will strengthen our sense of identity and make us less codependent. By being more aware of the subtle difference between codependency and compassion, we strengthen the one and reduce the other. It is win-win.

Seeing Ourselves in Others

Of the five steps of compassion, we have mostly been exploring the fourth step, the art and science of how to feel what others feel, but in practice, before we can get to the feeling part, we must first take the second step, which is to find a point of unity or commonality between you and another person.

I encourage you, then, to start your practice of compassion by focusing your efforts on *seeing yourself in other people*.

We are all children of the same God, and we all reflect the same Divine virtues, yet we spend most of our time looking at the things that set us apart from everyone else. When we look for differences, we find differences. But if we look for similarities, we quickly discover that we are all more alike than we are different.

See ye no strangers; rather see all men as friends, for love and unity come hard when ye fix your gaze on otherness.
— 'Abdu'l-Bahá

Trying to see yourself in the people around you is the first *conscious* step in the practice of compassion. Finding points of commonality will help you see things from their perspective. Seeing things from their perspective will help you understand their feelings about things. Understanding their feelings will provide opportunities for you to feel the same way that they feel, at least once in a while, and will move you to service. In the long run, it will make you more compassionate.

But you don't have to worry about the long run. Focus on finding positive similarities with every single person you meet—even if at first they are ridiculously shallow. *Ah, that* person has the same color of hair as I do, and that one buys the same brand of milk. That person laughs at the same jokes, and that one also has a child they love. Someone here is a writer, or at least speaks English. Is anyone here worried about global warming?

Start with the obvious, and keep going. Make it a game, or be completely serious. Just thinking about finding something in common with the people around you will change your entire perspective on life. On some deep level, it will connect you to the world.

Compassionate Service

What separates compassion from sympathy or empathy is that it is expressed through acts of kindness. When you begin to see yourself in others and feel what they feel, then *you are moved* to act in an appropriate way. This kindness rises from an inner knowing of what the other person needs, and an inner desire to *do unto others as you would have them do unto you.*

By putting compassion into action, you achieve the third goal of this book. The first is to heal emotional wounds. The second is to enjoy life more by experiencing positive emotional sensations. The third is to discover alternatives to unhealthy behaviors, because it is always easier to replace bad habits than to hide from them.

What can you *do* to find opportunities to practice compassionate service? How do you go from the abstract appreciation of the value of compassion to the actual face-to-face experience of it?

Note: Before you look at my list of suggestions, remember that you should not choose a population or activity that might trigger inappropriate or obsessive behavior. Whoever it is you are attracted to, *go serve someone else.*

At the risk of repeating myself, the first place to go might be to an appropriate twelve-step meeting. There you can practice honesty, forgiveness and compassion all at the same time. But there are many other fields of service you might want to consider as well.

You can start with your own family. Are there family members—adult or child—that you are taking for granted or even avoiding? Call them up or take them out and listen, listen, listen.

Are there members of your religious or social group who are alone, sick, or going through difficulties? Offer to help. Often the greatest service you can provide another person is to simply be there as a caring witness to the other person's experience, whether it is one of joy or grief.

Neighbors, hospitals, nursing homes, Big Brother, Big Sister, Scouts, soup kitchens, homeless shelters, Habitat for Humanity—the list of people and organizations that need your help is endless. Many cities have a non-profit volunteer coordinator or office that can direct you to an appropriate agency. Even if you are homebound yourself, you can make phone calls to shut-ins, send sympathy cards to the grieving, write letters to prisoners or soldiers, or say prayers for any and all of the above. I have a friend who stands in parking lots handing out stickers to children just to see them smile. She lives in a beautiful world.

Even the smallest act of service can change your focus from yourself and your problems to the needs of others. It may sound trite but it is true: the best way to help yourself is to help someone else.

*We have come to the last of our four tools of healing. This is the shortest section, not because faith is the least important, or because I have less to say about faith than the others, but because I have already written an entire book about the value of trusting in a loving God who allows us to suffer trials and tests in order to help us grow spiritually. That book is called **Why Me? A Spiritual Guide to Growing Through Tests**. If you believe in a God who is active in your life, then that book will be a great source of comfort and encouragement.*

This book, then, will look at a different aspect of faith— faith, not in an active God, but in the general goodness of the universe and in the security of our place within it.

Faith

The kind of faith you need for emotional healing does not involve a specific religion or doctrine. It isn't about holding on to dogma, or pledging love to one Messenger of God versus another. It is an attitude of trust in the general goodness of the universe, and a confidence that you have an important part to play. It is the kind of faith that speaks of purpose and meaning and belonging.

This kind of faith helps us overcome fear. Fear tells us that the world is unsafe, unstable and unfriendly. Faith tells us that the world is full of wonder, possibility and goodness. Without this kind of faith, we are predisposed to making a never-ending spiral of self-destructive choices that will hold us back for our entire lives. This is because having faith that everything will work out in the end—that there is enough good to go around and the world is on our side—does more than simply make us feel better or give us a sense of peace and hope, it also has a direct impact on our ability to control our impulses, resist temptation and delay gratification.

If you are not sure how having faith can help you control your impulses, delay gratification and make healthier decisions, let me describe some recent research that sheds some interesting light on the connection.

Researchers have known for decades that people who have trouble with controlling their impulses, or delaying gratification have a much harder time succeeding in life. They are more likely to do drugs, drop out of school, experience an unintended pregnancy, etc. Researchers know this because of a long-term follow-up study of children who participated in what is known as "The Marshmallow Test" at Stanford University in the 1960s. In it, researchers leave a four-year-old alone in a room with a single marshmallow or other treat and tell them that if they can wait until the researcher comes back in ten minutes to eat it, they can have TWO treats instead of one. Children who were good at this— who waited the longest without eating the treat—were found to be more successful in many areas of their life as they grew into adulthood.

The fact that this one test correlated with a long-term pattern of behavior seemed to indicate that it was exposing an innate character quality in these children. A child was either good at delaying gratification or he wasn't, and if he wasn't when the test was given, he would probably never be. This consistency suggested that an ability to wait for a greater good was somehow written into a child's DNA.

The fact that poor kids tended to do less well on this test was explained, not by their poverty, but by an inherited predisposition for irresponsible behavior and short-term thinking.

So where does faith come in? Well, about 50 years later, as it turns out.

In a 2012 study of 56 three-to-five-year-olds, researchers at University of Rochester found that children who experienced *reliable interactions* with a researcher immediately before the marshmallow experiment waited on average *four times longer* to eat the marshmallow than children who had an unreliable interaction.

For this new version of the study, children were given *two* activities. In the first activity, they were promised a reward if they did an art project as requested. After doing the project, half of the children were given the promised reward, and half were not. Later, this same researcher told them that if they waited to eat their marshmallow, they would get a second one.

The children who had faith that the researcher would do as he promised waited a mean time of twelve minutes, while those who expected the researcher to let them down waited a mean time of three minutes—only one quarter as long.

The ones waiting three minutes were not poorer, less bright, or less able to control their impulses. They had less *faith* that waiting would gain them any advantage.

They had *learned* from experience that promises are broken, people are unreliable, and pleasure should be grabbed while it is sitting in front of you. As one of the researchers said, "If you are used to getting things taken away from you, not waiting is the rational choice."

This new study provides strong evidence that the kids who lacked self-control in the '60s were probably living in unstable households *before* they ever walked through the door to take the test. Is it any wonder, then, that the follow-up studies found them to be less successful?

Many of us also grew up in unstable homes. Even if we had religious faith, we did not necessarily have faith that God and the universe were looking out for our best interests. The idea that there was plenty to go around never occurred to us. We expected to run out; we expected to be disappointed; we expected to be lied to; we sometimes even expected to be hurt and abused. These expectations were developed as a result of our interaction with those whom we should have been able to trust. As a corollary to these expectations, we also expected to fail, to have the rug pulled out from under us, and to be caught in an endless Catch 22 of bureaucratic gotchas.

The expectation that life will kick you when you are down creates a self-sabotaging attitude. Why study if you will never graduate? Why wait to have sex if you will never have a career? Why *not* take drugs, if they make you feel good now?

When we combine this expectation of failure with feelings of guilt and shame, it is not surprising that many of us go through our days subconsciously looking for proof that the world is out to get us. When that is what we expect to see, that is exactly what we find.

Today, for example, my proof that the world is out to get me is the fact that both my favorite coffee flavoring and my favorite style of facial tissues have been discontinued by the manufacturers. Could life get any worse? Well, yes, of course it could. And if I keep looking, I am perfectly capable of *making* it worse. But I have the option to use my free will and my conscious choice to start looking for the good instead.

If faith in the general goodness of the world is what it takes to keep from spiraling down into self-destruction, then we all need to work on developing a little faith, no matter what our childhood experiences taught us. I would like to break this kind of faith down into four different aspects, none of which involve a specific religion or doctrine. They aren't about holding on to a theological belief, or pledging love to one Messenger of God versus another. They are about reflecting an attitude.

These aspects of faith invite us to accept the possibility of a power in the universe greater than ourselves; maintain an attitude of openness to the unknown; anticipate the good; and trust that everything will work to the good in the long run.

Contemplating a Higher Power

Our early childhood experiences didn't just shake our faith in our parents and earthly sources of authority. By extension they also undermined our ability to believe in a loving, safe, predictable Higher Power. "Higher Power" is the phrase many people in twelve-step groups us instead of the word "God". Many of us need an alternate word because for us, the word "God" carries with it too many negative connotations.

In *The Secret of Emotions*, I explained that when we were children, our parents *were* our gods. If our parents were angry, we internalized an angry god. If they were unpredictable, being loving one minute and cruel the next, then our god was erratic. If they were judgmental, always finding fault with us, then our internal god was judging us and looking for a reason to punish us.

If we did not feel that our parents were on our side, looking out for our best interest and doing whatever they could to help us succeed, then we internalized more than just the belief that life was unfair—we believed that God Himself was working against us.

To a lesser degree, this belief was reinforced by our relationships with other sources of authority in our lives, such as teachers, clergy, police, and bureaucrats of all sorts.

Because of these negative associations with God, some of us rejected the idea of God entirely, while others continued to believe in God. Some of those who continued to believe worked doubly hard to please him, while others gave up and identified themselves with those damned to go to Hell.

No matter which of these paths you have taken, you have the opportunity now to change your relationship to your Higher Power. Understand that whether we are conscious of it or not, we *all* believe in a Higher Power of some sort. We are born helpless and dependent upon adults who had much more power than we did. We believe, to the very core of our subconscious beings, that there is a power outside of us that is greater than we are because we *experienced* such a power every day of our early lives. Our feelings of helplessness and powerlessness were therefore embedded in our emotional reality at birth. They were reinforced by at least 10-15 years of additional experiences during our childhood and youth. It would be unrealistic to think we could erase these feelings from our psyches. No matter what our head tells us, our hearts tell us that there is something bigger than us out there. It would do no good to engage in an intellectual argument with our hearts over whether or not there is a God. What we can do instead, is accept that our hearts will always long for a source of power, strength and protection, and then slowly redefine our Higher Power, both mentally and emotionally, to be more supportive and loving.

Whether we realize it or not, many of us currently have *faith* that things are going to fall apart on us. Whether we think of it as bad luck, bad karma, or punishment for our evil ways, we tend to expect the worst. With awareness, we can transform that negative faith into an anticipation of the good and trust that things really can work out.

We can start by simply maintaining an attitude of openness to the unknown.

Transforming our Faith

Fear of the unknown keeps us returning to *the Devil we know* rather than opening ourselves up to the Angels that we never dreamed existed. When we think we know how the universe really works, we project our past pain, abuse and failures into our future and then live up to our low expectations.

Faith means believing that things can be *different*—not *only* different, but different in ways we can't even begin to predict.

This attitude of openness to the unknown also helps counteract perfectionism. Perfectionism leaves us terrified of the unknown because it is outside of our control, and because to be perfect is to know everything that needs to be known. To be able to say, "I don't know, and that's OK," can open new paths of personal exploration.

Most of us live our lives on auto-pilot, putting one foot in front of the other in a predictable pattern, day in and day out. Faith invites us to look up, look around, and maybe, just *maybe*, veer off in a new direction. It also reminds us that it is OK to do this, and that the unknown can even be a safer, friendlier option than the step we normally take.

To be open to an unknown good allows us to take the next step of faith, which is to *anticipate* the good.

Anticipate the Good

This reminds me of the old bumper sticker, "Expect a Miracle!" I always felt that that was pretty damn demanding on my part. To expect something, to me, implies that someone else is going to provide it for you.

I decided I preferred the phrase, "anticipate blessings." Anticipation is a state of readiness. It implies an openness to what is possible, rather than a demand for what is impossible.

If I am open to seeing and receiving blessings, then I am more likely to recognize them when they arrive, yet there is no time limit on anticipation. Good things could come today, tomorrow or next year. But the feeling of anticipation is a positive one, full of hope and enthusiasm.

When we anticipate the good, it becomes easier to take the last step of faith:

Trust That Everything Will Work to the Good in the Long Run

In a world filled with pain and suffering, having faith that everything will be all right in the end may be the most difficult thing that I've asked you to do in this book. So let me offer you some perspectives to help you set aside fear and distrust and look forward to the future with faith and hope.

If we define "everything will be all right" as "I will live a long and prosperous life," then I cannot guarantee that you will get your heart's desire.

If, however, we define "all right" as "I will continue to grow and experience the joy of fulfilling my spiritual potential," then I can, with absolute confidence, assure you that you will find the good you seek.

The purpose of each individual's life is to become the best, most fully developed expression of that individual's potential that is possible. Or, to be more specific, the purpose of *your* life is to be the best *you* possible. This is achieved by developing your inner character qualities—*your* virtues—which in turn will heal your pain and bring you joy. No matter what life throws at you, you still have the choice to follow this path and live your potential. You don't need to have faith that the external world will be pleasant. You only need to have faith that whatever unpleasantness you experience will help you to grow.

The Power of Synergy

Honesty gives us the capacity to see what was missing.
Forgiveness gives us permission to speak it.
Compassion gives us the ability to understand it, and
Faith gives us the opportunity to turn it over to God.

I started this book by saying that I would tell you about four different tools of emotional healing. By now, however, you have probably figured out that these are not separate tools. They all work together with each other, and with every other virtue that your heart is anxiously waiting for the opportunity to develop.

Faith gives us the courage to be honest. Honest self-discovery helps us discover what we need to forgive, but it also shows us why we have so little faith. An attitude of forgiveness makes it easier to be honest with ourselves about what we have done and what those we love have done to us. Compassion helps us see situations through the eyes of those who hurt us, which makes them easier to forgive.

As we expand our capacity for each of these qualities, we enter an expanding spiral of growth. Each step forward in any area opens up new possibilities in all areas.

And it is not just these four qualities that will be strengthened. Faith builds courage and courage releases creativity. Creativity generates enthusiasm. Enthusiasm replaces anger as the energizing force behind our actions.

Honesty builds trustworthiness, which reinforces nobility, which creates confidence which releases joy.

The connections never end.

No matter where you start; no matter what qualities you decide to develop, you will begin to fill, one by one, all of the empty spaces in your heart, and heal the wounds you thought could never be healed. You were created to be whole. It is what you are destined to be. Whether it takes a year or a lifetime, you will achieve it.

Have faith.

An Introduction to Book 3:

Longing for Love

In book 3, we take what we have learned about the nature of our emotions and apply it to the practical goal of recognizing, building and keeping healthy relationships. The first half of the book focuses on preparing ourselves to recognize true love, as opposed to the many substitute emotions that draw us into relationships, including fear, shame, need, pity, attachment and loneliness. The second half addresses the many temptations that can sabotage a relationship once it has begun.

Here are some of the headings in this book to give you an idea of what will be addressed:

Part 1 How Do I Find the Right Person?
Intimate Friendships
How to Recognize Virtues in Others
Loneliness and Anxiety
Other Basic Advice for the Search
Choosing Intimacy over Intensity
Other Sensations We Mistake for Love
Building a Healthy Relationship
Part 2 Dealing with Temptation
Resisting Unhealthy Behaviors
Practical Advice for Dealing with Attractions
Dealing with Inappropriate Desires
The Power of Denial

Available from:
SecretofEmotions.com and Amazon.com

About the Author

Justice Saint Rain is the author of several books that blend psychology with spiritual insights. He is both a writer and an artist, and has been producing a line of spiritually-oriented material for over 30 years. He currently lives with his family on a farm in Southern Indiana.

He does not do life-coaching or consultations by phone or e-mail, but he does have a FaceBook page called *Love, Lust and the Longing for God*, an author's page at GoodReads.com and a writer's blog.

He will be happy to try to answer questions and respond to comments posted at any of these sites.

Join the conversation at:
www.justicesaintrain.com

Made in the USA
Columbia, SC
02 April 2021